BROKEN SLEEP BO

Edited b

ISBN: 978-1-913642-14-3

Book designed by Aaron Kent

Edited by Aaron Kent

Broken Sleep Books (2020), Talgarreg, Wales

Contents

Poetry

Non-Fiction

Broken Sleep Books 2020

Edited by: Aaron Kent

Poetry

macular degenerate

Emilee Moyce

17/01/2020

Over the Moon

Last night, I swam over the moon.
I was so afraid of time, so scared
of ageing, that I jumped
into the icy pacific depths
and I swam and swam.

The moon drew in closer, as
if through a telescope, zooming
nearer to my eyes which were
burning from the salt,
            from exhaustion,
            from crying.
I kept swimming until I lost sight
of land.

The water rose up
            and engulfed the moon.
                        I swam over it.

The shining pale blue disc
glowed at me from below,
illuminating the creatures
who swam alongside it.
Natural, peaceful –
as if the moon has always lived
just below the surface of the sea.

I turned to see if it had been an optical illusion,
but no, there it was – gently rising out of the water.
Softly, as not to make a sound.
Droplets danced along its bright, cratered surface.

I glanced over my shoulder
to watch the moon rise;
to see it settle back in its cradle
high above the earth.

Soon my fingers touched sand
as I crawled out of the sea.
It didn't matter where I had landed.
I was still afraid of time, still
scared of ageing. But I found a
place to rest my head and I felt
that I was floating –
                    above the world
                    or in its bluest depths,
                    or both at the same time.

I felt that I was floating,
my eyes no longer burned, and I slept
until the sun came and went away again,
waking only when the moon called my name.

Fallbrook

I drove to the big yellow house
on the edge of suburban sanity;
it looks different than it does in my dreams.
Next door, there used to be a field
of fresh possibility – there used to be life
among the leaves and grass,
but new settlement has squashed it.

The feeling has changed.
A felled tree, a pot of paint,
brand new carpet, bleached stains –
this is a house now, not home.

I hear laughter echoing in twenty rooms:
the sound of youth and progress.
I thought my breath gave life,
but home has its own lungs.

I leave a note in the mailbox
to those who now rest their heads
where I once slept so soundly.
'I hope you don't mind,' I write,
'that my subconscious crawls
up the stairs every night.
I try to be quiet; just a spectre
hugging the walls, hearing
the laughter that came before.'

I still see it all in my dreams.
As I drive away, I imagine
that nothing has changed.
I know those walls remember me.

A jewelry box, a costume dress,
a lingering song of emptiness,
dinosaur tracks and childhood fears –
they still live there through all the years.

Budgeting

How do you quantify sight?
Should it be in minutes
moments
molecules?
How do you count the uncountable?

The sand in the hourglass
is making no attempt to fight
the gravity that pulls it to the bottom.
Whatever this currency is,
I am spending it foolishly.

I spend hours staring at the same white walls,
too much time letting LED light transfix me.
Not enough time loving every earthly texture.

The dollars in this wallet are dwindling;
I am letting them float away on the breeze.

I could count and count and recount forever.
No amount of time would ever be enough.

Paper Cranes

Paper cranes never granted me any wishes.
They only stole delicate lines of fingerprints
and nights of restful sleep, patience testing me.

I've folded dozens of happy marriages,
strung up a few prosperous and peaceful lives,
but I never surrendered my own sacrifice
to the paper gods in return for my own wish.

I'm not even sure what I'd ask for if I did.
Perhaps not to rot in a landfill years from now
as I'm sure some of my lovely birds are doing,
their beaks crushed under bags of filth and needless waste.

Maybe I'd wish not to have my wings ripped and clipped,
not to be stowed away, a fading memory
gathering dust in a box where the sun can't reach.

Or maybe I'd try to be a bit less selfish
and wish for the world to find some kind of order,
but I think futility would halt my fingers
and I'd give up before I made the thousandth fold.

I suppose I'd wish for light and vibrant colour.
For warming sun and for the strength to stretch my wings.
But it never felt right to put forth my own hope –
it's far easier to grant others' wishes than your own.

m cul r degener te

c n you open your eyes little wider?
c n you see this red colour?
red like stop like b d like blood
 re you sensitive to light?

c n you re d the next line?
h ve you recently been hit in the he d?
h ve you h d ny eye infections?
h ve you done tests like these before?

wh t questions do you h ve for me?

my questions h ve no nswers/
i sit mongst elders who st re
 nd judge me for my blue h ir
blue like screens th t they think
h ve m de me blind
blue like skies th t neither of us
c n see with n ked eyes

i get no f vours from my young ge
 s every word on every p ge
h s to go through screening process
to be dmitted into my visu l field

cl rity is unobt in ble
the nswer lies in blood s mples –
my retin l cells re dying
centr l vision f ding f st

the octogen ri ns c n tut and sigh
but they re the lucky ones
with eighty ye rs of perfect sight
while i w it for the d rk to come
wondering wh t i will be ble to see

when i turn thirty

i count the st rs in the sky every night
but l tely, i c n’t sep r te
the fl shes nd blinks
from the st rs in my own eyes

i feel t home in the retin l clinic/
i m   m cul r degener te.

Out, Voyage

Jaydn DeWald

31/01/2020

Arrangement, Nuclear

We discovered our house was spheroid, like the earth.
Our beds were afloat on moonlit carpets.
Our daughter feverishly drawing circles in black crayon on butcher paper—did she think she was stirring a potion, generating a storm?
I used to write poems ending with lone boats creaking at sundown.
All winter we perched on stools in our garage, piecing together scorched-edged shreds of a map.
Our son gently pulled our eyelashes, or he squirmed his hands inside our mouths as though we were sock puppets.
Suddenly a dark wave of laundry crashed over us.
I closed my eyes, I listened to womb noises, I tasted burnt toast in the air.
Like the earth, too, our house was rotating.
My partner wore a long sheer nightgown that she swished around and around until she disappeared—

Past Developing

Forget the waitress who resembled Sappho.
The salt cod she served us drifted like sand
Between the tines of our forks. On the tube
Sat children painting little clay St. Jeromes,
But even that light made her cheeks glisten.
"I'm greener than the grass is green," I said,
And raised the centuries-old wine that had
Our heads spinning. I dreamt of the Gorilla
Suit I wore in college—the darkness inside.
Behind the bar stood the rotted, black mast
To which Odysseus had been tied. And yet
Its placard: *None of this is being preserved*
Via video surveillance. Our hunk of peasant
Bread. Those paper placemats. Plates of oil.
We carried around our necks huge Polaroid
Cameras, so there was no use remembering.
Through red window curtains, light caught
Us red-handed, napkins rising to our noses.
On the specials chalkboard, the old barman
Playing Hangman. One leg. No I's. No face.

Voyage Out

He's standing beside his hammock, above his sleeping body, which dreams of stumbling along an ever-winding path of leaves & ashes, when a distant, quavering soprano begins to sing—a voice he'd heard, years before, on a bronze hill overlooking the ocean, & ever since regretted not searching for, not hurtling toward her in the rubescent dusk of summer, tearing off his rucksack. "Wake up," he tells his body, nudging its shoulder with his knee. But it goes on lying there, an enormous baby in a sling, because it is dying in its sleep: it has collapsed on the dark path among the scraping leaves, watching his twelve-year-old daughter in her plum-black dress (so like a dream within a dream) stumble forward in its place. He runs his hand over the blond hairs of its forearm. Then he stares up at the white light through the lemon trees & at his daughter dancing, one rainy evening, before the old projector, the old faces of relatives (contorted, celery-green) streaked across her flannel PJs. What can account for this desire to hurtle out into the streets, to find the soprano's voice, rising again, in the paling distance? *Art thou a little spirit bearing up a corpse*, as Epictetus said, or is the soprano tempting him—like an egret on a thin branch—to leave, to let the body go? His daughter, at the beach with some friends, in the tarantualic shadow of a palm tree, will no doubt walk, hours later, over the damp grass toward his body, then suddenly freeze in the middle of the yard—warm & windless & the moon in her salt-hardened hair—noticing a smudge of white, the peak of his nose, above the hammock. Now he's touching for the last time (as his daughter will, crumpling to her knees) the paper eyelids, the colorless lips & ill-shaven chin. O how he's dreamt of the soprano silhouetted on an ice floe, of lurching toward her through rags of swirling snow, burning to see her, to watch her sing! Soon his daughter, as she replaced his body in its dream, will be standing right here in this place before the hammock, trying again & again to shape these wooden fingers around her tiny hand—although by then, of course, he will be long gone, loping across violet sands, searching for the soprano: the quavering voice, the painted mouth . . .

Sleeping Lions

the willing giving over of the self to the other, to power
—Jack Halberstam

When I arrived, around noon, at the Blue Danube Café,
A plump gentleman clambered up out of his pink chair
Begging me to take his seat, please, sit down, sit down.
My feet tingled. "Splendid," I said. Another large man
Began to take my arms out of my coat. "Ahead of time,
As usual," said a petite woman, seated across from me,
Lifting her demitasse. She seemed to resemble a figure
From my deepest past. A hand was placed on my knee.
A pale hand on my dark trousers. A girl, in front of me,
Asking me what I should like to order. "Coffee, strong,"
I said. A faint, meaningful light haunted the blank wall
Behind the counter. A woman beside the petite woman
Said: "Oh, dear, you must be tired," and, indeed, I was

Half asleep. My mother hung above me, tucking me in,
Pulling the white sheet up over my face. "I'm fatigued,"
I told the woman, though she had long since moved on
To wittier conversation. "How ambitious he used to be,"
Said a young chap staring down at me. "What a waste,"
His friend agreed. In a circular mirror, on the side wall,
The whitest snow fell. My porcelain cup of cold coffee
Sloshed about in my lap as if I was driving somewhere
To the din of battle drums. Still, I was courteously still.
"He seems, well, *excited*," said a tanned young woman,
Coming right up to my face. A couple of bookish boys
Stood watching. "I wouldn't do that," one of them said,
Grimacing. "No," said the other. "I think that's enough."

Our Pillar

Our son toddled around
In my *Moby-Dick* shirt. Our daughter
Was a bruise-colored blanket
Tumbling from her bed to the floor.
We gathered stuffed animals
In our arms, or we took turns
Spacing out in front of the coffee-
maker. I wrote a poem
About a green ribbon falling
From an egret's beak. One minute
We heard them snoring to
Earth, Wind & Fire; the next
They were squatting on our chests
And gnawing slobberingly
At our fingers. You say,
They meow at sunset, they ooze like mist
Across our floors, they definitely
Have wings. One of them locked us
In the bathroom, the other
Busted us right out. We were
Archaeologists searching for a fabled
Wooden block. Our hands
Glided side by side into the
Darkness under the sofa
Like swans. Remember the end
Of Kafka's "The Bucket Rider"
When the narrator *ascends*
Into the regions of the ice mountains
And is lost forever? Our daughter
Pointed down the hall, to a path
Of floral-print cushions . . .

What we say is home

Arpit Kaushik

17/02/2020

Express Journey

The red-bricked clock tower in Delhi
announces my arrival, soon I will board a train

for the four-day journey to Assam
My nappies will dry on the window grill

and then I will go to find my first bicycle
in Nangal, root my childhood complexes

before dashing to a high rise in Bombay
where I will idolise Amitabh Bachchan and

drive in a Fiat for four days across Thar desert
to my grandfather's village in Delhi

I will fly away from him to the garden city
of Bangalore, eat *Dosas* and *Idlis*, get good grades

take a bus to the desert town of Pilani where
I will make lifelong friends, drink, smoke, party

become an engineer and start a job in Delhi
then make it to Hyderabad to study some more

and move to Bangalore to start climbing the ladder,
erase thoughts of past loves, get married

and move abroad to start a new life in Reading
fail in business, then reboot in London

Here I will change my children's nappies, start
a new job, find a voice, write these words.

Rakhi

Rakhi is an annual festival celebrated in India to honour the brother-sister relationship

Awakened in the morning
by mother's voice saying
get ready, they get ready.

In front of the altar – a steel tray,
clay lamp, vermillion powder,
dried rice grains, water, sweets

and the ornamental thread – Rakhi,
outshining mirrors, mosaics, beads:
the sister's red and yellow dress.

She makes a paste of powder,
dots and stretches it on his head,
plasters some grains, lights the lamp,

circles the tray around his face,
ties the Rakhi on his wrist and
says a prayer. He vows to protect her.

The sweet. His hand. Her mouth.
That same sweet. Her hand. His mouth.
The cash envelope, a photograph.

Thirty years later, they are between
Delhi and London. The Rakhi
arrives by post. He files it

On the day, they talk, their lives,
their kids, then he takes out the Rakhi,
ties it with his mouth, says a prayer.

Patta

Patta is a type of cloth typically worn by lower classes in villages of North India

In Indian summers on a cane chair,
he sits with a hand fan, driving away flies.
Gravity pulls sweat from his brow, neck, chest,
trying in vain to dissolve *Hanuman,*
the monkey god on his thigh.

Stipes of cerulean, cobalt, navy
in wholesale cotton –
my grandfather's boxers – mid-waisted,
draw-stringed, held halfway to knee.

My tiny *phathar-phatar* footsteps,
rubber *chappals* rebounding off sandstone
break the flow of silence. He rises,
lifts me up, rests me on his thigh,
"My prince" he says as I slip
from the proud *patta* I never felt
on a living person again.

Pilani

When peacocks screamed at dusk
drowning the sound of ringing bells
on handlebars of rusted bicycles
that pedalled homewards.

When I rummaged through the pile
of unclaimed letters by the window
reading the same addresses
hoping to find that one letter for me.

When I queued up in the phone booth
"All lines in this route are busy,
please try later", a price to pay for
a connection not worth waiting for.

When the wrapped *chowkidars*
suddenly surfaced from dark corners
of the alley next to the library
where you and I always met.

Pilani Reunion

Our bus starts late from Delhi.
Sam and Surdie wind me up:
speak to your past crush,
look there she is. I go and sit down
next to her, the soundtrack
changes to retro Bollywood romance,
all passengers sway their arms,
someone waves her *dupatta.*
I sink further into my seat.

Six hours later we reach Pilani.
As the bus crosses the campus gate
we burst into our old theme song,
then retrace our steps, walking
in the middle of dusty paths –
it's the bird shit we have to avoid.
We reach the garden café,
the moss layered pond where
we dunked birthday boys,

then order our usual *chai* and puff.
We stand still, breathing in
the wintry sunset, walking again
through the academic block:
its corridors now dark, lime-washed.
We reach our old hostel rooms,
comment on how the iron grills
make the hostel seem like a prison,
how the bogs have been upgraded,

now with running hot water,
western style commode. We say hello
to the current students in their
millennial look – fit, bearded, spectacled.
We go to the food shack, *Nagarji ki Redi,*

order a *samosa chaat* and *kela-rabri,*
roll a joint and smoke, channelling
every oscillation in fluorescent light,
flapping our wings, us mere beings.

Love and/or the storm

Jonny Wiles

29/02/2020

To a Rock

This burial is of the gentlest kind,
the easiest of all things to unearth.
One heave of stone and muscle will reverse
the sinking weight of beach. And so you find,
out on this farthest limb, there rests a thing
whose very stillness is a violence
the water's breathing contours cant hold in,
nor can it could the damage the event
of motionlessness might inflict. You see,
although the mass would speak, if speak it could,
movement is all that can be understood
out here. Listen: *ricorditi di me*
no more than this, and this is nothing, and
the utter fact of this unmoving sand.

dedalus

it's supposed to fit tightly so that you can bear the lightness
it's been crafted with love for your own shoulders
let me clip this little history across your back
so much of it is bird pure bird ah your child
-ren's children will hold it so dear
so now strap it over your neck
draw it shut like
a buckle

perhaps the wind has a language if it does we will speak it
it must have a word for FLY it will sing it only to us
hell son they'll see us for miles over
only let there be no way no *modo di dire*
to say *this is him this is that man*
who is the wax
is the heat

the water

lines from voicemail

1. hello, we've been trying to contact you

2. how much of last night do you remember?

3. i'm calling to answer some of your questions

4. if that's something that interests you

5. it's not urgent yet, but

6. let's say sooner rather than later

7.

8. no i don't think he's there

9. anyway, that's all I wanted to say

10. and it'd be great to see you later

11. get back to me when you can

12. everything's alright

13. i love you

14. please hang up

fragment. 2009.

[silent
willows]

haiku on the movement of time

[unfinished]

be

[ ] come back

away

Three Spiders Fucking

Robin Purves

17/03/2020

On Earth it means an opening in a house, a door, or a place on the forest floor that lets light in. It means daybreak, and the incandescent lantern, burning magnesium in the smoke hole. A luminous glade with a pale, bright flame. White spots in the eye, kindling, interior lux. Perhaps also atonement, and victims brought to light.

Make a perforation in the plaintext for this person, or for this person, or for this person: start from there. Being as close as possible to them, being beside them, will make them feel good when you and those persons stay passionate and so on. A person's morning is happy, when a person facing a person, or facing the morning happiness of a person, is happy.

He told himself he
could turn round would look
back he would see her again

Then everything was not
there: no way and
no place and no other earth,
no sun and no sky,

He turned round
sweating a skilful
kiss goodbye and

Like another earth
everything was there again:
the way and the place,
he could see

On the way to a tree
guess what:

Dead love is in the frame then
you hold tight and cheat yourself.

He took his scarf and
folded it against
rocks forest a bridge
and a sweet, long-suffering sky
hung over this blind basin
in pale stripes.

Hang there,

Do not go away. The throat
that you flirt with
in the shadow
of a head or an end
without passion will
be

Dead in the year. You
go on without me, to the

empty socks.

Go to bed.
A man in a blue coat
has eaten the way.

Or just as often the flame goes out
and a man is hanging from a bough in a clearing
his blue coat off in
And the trees close as
all the streaming services close.

The dog was agitated when
I reached the clearing I saw
the ruin, a dead man is like
a baby, you hold it
where it's not bleeding

I found you here and
then I looked for you

Faded green T-shirt
from which birds spring

Yellow eyelid the
eyeballs ripened

In the sky the
hot pink ball gag sun

In addition tonight you see
the scaffold hemp scarf

The flowering jade balance
a perfume could upset

Climbing spirits in the flask
the person from the hanging scroll

now gone in weighted
sack to the forest floor

Half-sitting in the neck of the wood
the operation wilts

The grass soaks up you know what
the flow of gold soft water

Has nothing to do
with this planet

At the bend of a path
and a needle-strewn bed
the sun shone on rot,
and the rot from the bed
looked at the sun.

After a long walk in
wet shoes, a dead man
spreads.

Collar in the cress,
he lies under the clouds
pale in his green bed, the
light is drizzling.

He is dead, his
hand on his shirt,

Withering tissues of the heart
of the foot come out

of the boot, the ankle moth
bitten fly symmetry

In the pines
a mile and a
half from here
I found you
and then I looked for you,
still in a tree:
throw the T-shirt aside
there slipped off
in the branches
destroy everything,
to the roots

The dragonfly taper touched
wings and made for the exit

infra·structure

Katy Lewis Hood
&
Maria Sledmere

31/03/2020

Darkland

Ordinance rent
at basic scales
full ease with oil
all over the docks

oasis is better
to fill the throat
these railways sleep
telluric still

Investing a cloud
lightly of pesticide
in red-eye night

by uncanny fingers
to carry no scars
of noxious current

Unborn in Forth
attuned to our city
backwards the land

other works remain
prone to melt
locks itself

ordinance itself:
rent locks oasis land
is the better backwards
at melt basic to scales
prone to city fill our
~~the to~~ throat attuned
full remain ease works
with other oil
these Forth railways
in sleep unborn
all current over noxious
~~the of~~ docks telluric
night still red-eye
investing scars no a cloud
carry ~~by to~~ pesticide
uncanny of fingers
lightly

Divers

the basin a haw this a.m., sky eyedropped
the contrails, made retrofit light. of burning:
bed nooked into wall and half the grey
matter still awake when exhaust subsides

into elbow, old name for constants of shifting
baselines overhead—hypnagogic tracks
in bitumen lines. dreamt sweeping membrane
over debris, memory of pump installation

bedded in, built around, multiple units
pass electric a blink. always the energetic
question going backwards and backwards
until conservative by proxy, we sit on

our hands. looped converting work to heat,
firmament nests matte. at a given height,
a bird's eye is taken as given as invitation
for tenders, networked proximity or virtual

shaking, palm clamped too slow convexed
over lens. the fruiting season: model
windfall of a plane would fly like a draining
of fluid carbon fixing, evolutions ago

the basin a.m., eyedropped

retrofit.

bedwall grey

awake when

elbow for constants

hypnagogic

in bitumen membrane

over debris installation

bedded in multiple units

electric a blink

going backwards and backwards

by proxy

looped ~~converting~~ work to heat,

firmament matte

invitation

for tenders

shaking, palm convexed

over lens. the fruiting

windfall

of fluid ~~carbon~~ fixing, evolutions ago

Hydrogalvanic

a cycle of nerves. a siting submerged
in the current state of searching for patience,
otherwise patents of the cellular type.

care as unmet precondition for the alkaline
body in refracted light bodied of water,
buoyed between countries, clashing

currency and hearts. electrified sounding
stone, net of inventions a tent in the motions
of wavework takes a generation outliving

itself as domestic collapse. pay fountains
down, stagnates at flash of a bulb: animal,
detector, electrolyte. in the town across

the water, the women sit plenteously
given to flow, circuitous motion a spark
in the channel, which parts and parts.

first leg of experiment—kickback, cathodic—
corrosion is steady, directive, intact.
the trajectory of the dammed is a man-

camp evaporating the porous, breaking
out static and sweat for inflammatory, cut-
and-dried conduit powering up lines and lines.

a
cycle
of
nerves
a
siting
submerged
in
the
current
state
of
searching
for
patience
otherwise
patents
of
the
cellular
type
care
as
unmet
precondition
for
the
alkaline

body
in
refracted
light
bodied
of
water
buoyed
between
countries
clashing
currency
and
hearts
electrified
sounding
stone
net
of
inventions
a
tent
in
the
motions
of
wavework
takes

a
generation
outliving
itself
as
domestic
collapse
pay
fountains
down
stagnates
at
flash
of
a
bulb
animal
detector
electrolyte
in
the
town
across
the
water
the
women
sit

plenteously
given
to
flow
circuitous
motion
a
spark
in
the
channel
which
parts
and
parts
first
leg
of
experiment
kickback
cathodic
corrosion
is
steady
directive
intact
the
trajectory

of
the
dammed
is
a
man
camp
evaporating
the
porous
breaking
out
static
and
sweat
for
inflamma-
tory
cut
and
dried
conduit
powering
up
lines
and
lines

These Queer Mermen

Serge Neptune

17/04/2020

A Mermen Choir: How we First came to Land

human experience is one of
disease you wouldn't remember us
first crawling out of water
panting for air in fierce
spasms the pain we knew
water no longer being our
mother giving up our gills
and growing porous bags to
breath swapping our one extremity
for two less silver and
more skin found refuge in
cracked lumps in the darkness
of the ground then behold –
our looks of wonder when
facing the first leap of flame

And if we Wanted to Perambulate like Humans do

The potion they served us, like surgeons,
cut through our blood with irons,
parted our spine like a vision of saints.

Beloved, if only you knew, how my fishtail
splits for you with this desire I can no longer name,
how its sword slashes me into two weaker halves.

Scales would fall, fins harden into bones.
Each step felt like a pig's heart skewered with nails,
like putting one's sole on a carpet of blades.

In the end we discovered our princes as whimsical,
how freedom made them rainbow-feathered birds
that leap from rose to lily without a care.

A Child Comes Out as a Merman

When right after sunset darkness landed on our living room
like a butterfly on an open flower,
mother didn't bother to switch on the lights
and kept watching the telly, laid on our sofa.
The telly blasting *SINNERS! SINNERS!*
While standing by the threshold to the kitchen,
I announced – my voice all jelly – *I am a merman now!*
and mother looked at me for a second, nodded
and tucked her lips again into a blanket of silence.
The morning after I found a leaflet next to my pillow,
content I could not decipher, with pictures as bright
as sun-filled bubbles of morality. Mother said
if I wanted to learn how to swim, they'd pay for lessons.
Dad in the car pestered me with lectures about being
only thirteen and knowing nothing, being full of nothing.
You shall not lie with a creature of the sea, for they have no soul
and only by marrying a creature of land, may they acquire one
I started taking baths before sleep and went to bed
so wet I'd soak the sheets.
Then started sleeping in the bathtub all night.
I joined my legs tight with an elastic band,
enjoyed every cramp, every cold shiver.
The next day screams and thumps out of the bathroom door
woke me up, as I delayed everyone's morning routine.
Over breakfast, mother insisted, once more, I was clueless.
I said I'd found a new god, one more tender,
one that allowed for mellowness.
Mother shook her head, dad shouted to go to my room,
called me an abomination.
I refused to eat their food, I asked mother to cook seaweed.
They decided to leave me alone, a shadow sewing
button-eyes on ghost dolls. No one took a bath in the evening.
They noticed me less and less.
Once, they watched a stand-up show on the telly, had their chests
shake with so much laughter, they couldn't hear a thing.
Once the water in my bathtub was all cherry, I tried to stop
the flowers of my wrists from blossoming.

A Mermen Choir: Let a Tap Left Dripping Overnight

be our lovesong
no death is sweeter
than a death in our arms
man of land man
of many labours
remember the younger
days discovering
the frailties of
your body
the embarrassment
of communal showers
those pressured
tiny licks like
hands touching
every inch of skin
even now you dream
the same dream
or maybe you're literally
sinking
our lips
grazing yours
our tongues pushed
down your throat
quite forcefully
like water flooding
the collapsing
temple of yourself

The Beginning of Dawn

In those thin hours when night sheds
its worm skin, its polluted armour,

when lamplights switch off and go home
to some hypothetical realm of lamplights,

when amber wrestles with rose
and dampens the sky with colour, in a city

that once whispered *I love you* the same way he did
on a ferry boat sulking on the Thames.

Aprire

Gemma Jackson

30/04/2020

heard once about a man
cut him
self open to
sag jaws [they]
say this: you are 2 moons full
&
it's just a phase
bookwalled-like and tongued touch where the sou
nd was meant to go breathing witness shaped bodyslates
exhale.
unassimilated intrusions are the sexy kind muted
stirrings fluidly/so fluidy/so.much.fluid. wet enough for mama-pecks
& clean sides in case [they] ask
something she might grow into.

you don't have to say it that way/do you/say it/that/way of saying
collarbones are for chumps anyway of saying is this expressive/wide
enough staged in cardboard angles last seen pouring herself through the
cracks in [their] back teeth a phantasmatic tracing told [them]:

first, she crawled.

stuffing the mouth, next, was a purely aesthetic study
those bee-sting globs only palatable with speed
& you there
fisting gums. all knuckle-pulp
& echoes

in the gentler version there are sister-shaped cotton lungs
& she calls it a verb and bullshit.

now this thing that you rest your wrists on is pink and squishy
maybe there's something in that too
grief ritualised
with this need to always be attached asking
what colour do you need to serve femme realness
to occupy space

sick of awareness. afflicting your own by eating breakfast for lunch
again to fuck up the space time continuum after correcting your tendency
to put mums where they don't belong.

turned to astrology as a last result for these ebbs and flows. it told you the
stars gave you a profound need for lists.

found a medusa on the table that was too big for pockets.

ate day long fruit all day for softer insides.

asked what it required. [they] replied “what”.

made a general gesture of writing down the significance of that.

screamed her head into the world.

at what point do we address the   room?

feels more honest to hold her in paint.

rejecting displays of unresolved somethings.

[they] express in our stomachs now.

in jasmine corners, always swallowing.

this is meant to be hopeful in a way, with the right standpoint.

told her you squeezed it right out
without making this a strip tease
except the clothes are wet
and there aren't any clothes
because we're naked and crying.

is this your way
of forcing her into representation
lined transpersonal: a consequence
of expressive limits and ambiguous bone structures
left cheek leaning more in your favour

write a muscle right out like that
let them think you've been chewing that biro, god
you are always chewing that biro like
no one told you

bred habitually sexed-up-like
of course clomping involves sideways dips and canines
more stringy choreography: imagine colour
tacked in the gaps you made

this was never a conversation
for the woman who gave you pages
from spotty signal
and pretend lingua-deafness.

Café Kaput!

Barney Ashton-Bullock

17/05/2020

Joggers

The strewn, stricken, jilted joggers
befilthed, enlittering encrusted carpets
and I smunch / trawl through the gaits and girths of all
in scuba search of the pearls conched within
of turdy streaked keks and jammy socks
to boil wash
such is my glee to be
a licky, licky retriever
getting a modicum of affirmation for such things
as lubricant to scant pleasantries
instead of unfathomable, distancing, mood swings
from Sir Lazyass about how I don't do a fukkin' thing

the swing an' bulge of his genital flopsies
seems to be his raison d'être
along with his untrue conceit
that no-one could love or fuck me better
and my raison d'être… oh, to help him forget her

The Bros of UnMersey

Mssrs doing smash-grab, slow-grip, throat choker thing;
A slappety mouth, yappety, yobbety, mugging, mauling!
Spent puffball, buffed-up flabster queens hithered,
Soon skittling as guttered scum a-flailing;
Stomped bauble beauties 'midst mirthy me-ow drawlings!

Cross fade to coke-stoked guffaws of tomcats' serrating screechios,
Cracked falsetto jubilations, clawing out mugged Muggins purse
Their wallets liberated to prolong team libation.

"20 quid more for a glam-slam gram fellas!"
Face slasher scowls abound afore:
Hearsehole fundament bootings as a jacksy's lubing
Prior to t'taunting,*"wanna taste fistings?"*
Enfrazzed in frenzied whippety
Pre and selfie-posing post coital cursings…

"Fukkin' reaped it!"
A shared cigarette
A mulched Mayo chip 'n' dip pack-munched

Blood soaked splotching on four quid throwaway Primark shirts
Worn from the cellophane without ironing
Used as offal bibs in sequential alley fuck'n'chuck fightings
Chocked and clocked, the slain's feint fearsome weeping
And to think such thuguli e'er made love to anything
Or that any young man bought them drinks hoping…

Sezincote

I've measured my days in summer fêtes that fade,
Annual tombolas, a Stromboli of remembrance;
The cheese, the wine, the bracelets we won,
As in another life, my Cotswolds one.

Apple-bobbing, mirth filled miscreants,
A tour of the grand house; *"No heels on the parquet!*
No fingers on the paintings!
And stay, if you will, on the carpet protectors!
And the banquettes are antiques and not for lounging,
Though the velveteen sheen does seem inviting!"

"The historic collection of monogrammed decanters are over there to view
With the family crested canteens of cutlery,
And much elbow grease needed to clean that lot, fuck you!"

The Orangery where we ate homemade cake and drank wan tea,
Where the maitre'd overheard my hashed plea
That I thought it best you marry me.

You, flustered that our fête-won, wax encased prize cheese,
Of which there were three in a Fine Fare presentation box,
Might soon get hot, were we not
To wend our way back to the train;
It was, thus, you'd skirt mention of my heart's intention
And I knew we'd not see Sezincote again.

Volte-Face (About Face)

Psoriasis of the sphincter
put an end to the chirrup of wild abandon
lest one eczmatic lava crack erupt
the folds of bloodied cack attack again
and the stench corrupt the fragrant windwhistles
into stormy eclectic invective

I'll stay unslain
snugly bound in my 2-for-1 chainstore knickers
slathered discreetly beneath
with Canestan and Daktacort
to ameliorate whatever
my fair slut bucket's re-caught
by means of the naïveté that's totally defined me
as so invert introvert, so inert

A supplicant initiate
to the wanton users of a world perverse
their daisy-chain, dick chase of flophouse flip-arse without a face
sidelined anew, crimped of night urges, I slur homeward
I slobber to shivering mother how, *"I will not be a mistake"*
she sips her cup-a-soup and stokes the trash in the grate

She burrs I be;
"stricken in a porno stew of old roux
that you do
too greatly stir, young sir"

Unpinned niche erotica adrift in vortices of pixel rifts
That radiate their briney starburst pfaffs 'cross dying screens
Such modem brokered bit torrent dreams veneer this unkempt mind
It's fitful digital flak scouring its rapidity of protraction
Misshapes form in the static and dissolve,

Shapeshifters, emergent, decay before they bless
To lead I, their tethered charge, to a broken righteousness
Through corridors of the lie, *"Volte-face"* (about face)

i pray from god my soul escapes

an expansive, cinematic bravado;
bawdy, iambic, barrack mess banter.
the assertive chivalry of opening bottles on molars:
human vassal states in klonky sidewalk *'klompendanse'.*

"lovely stag attire, cunt:
could do with a splash more colour!"
and sabre cuts a skein of ruby red
around a radial arc of neck.

Dorothy

Briony Hughes

31/05/2020

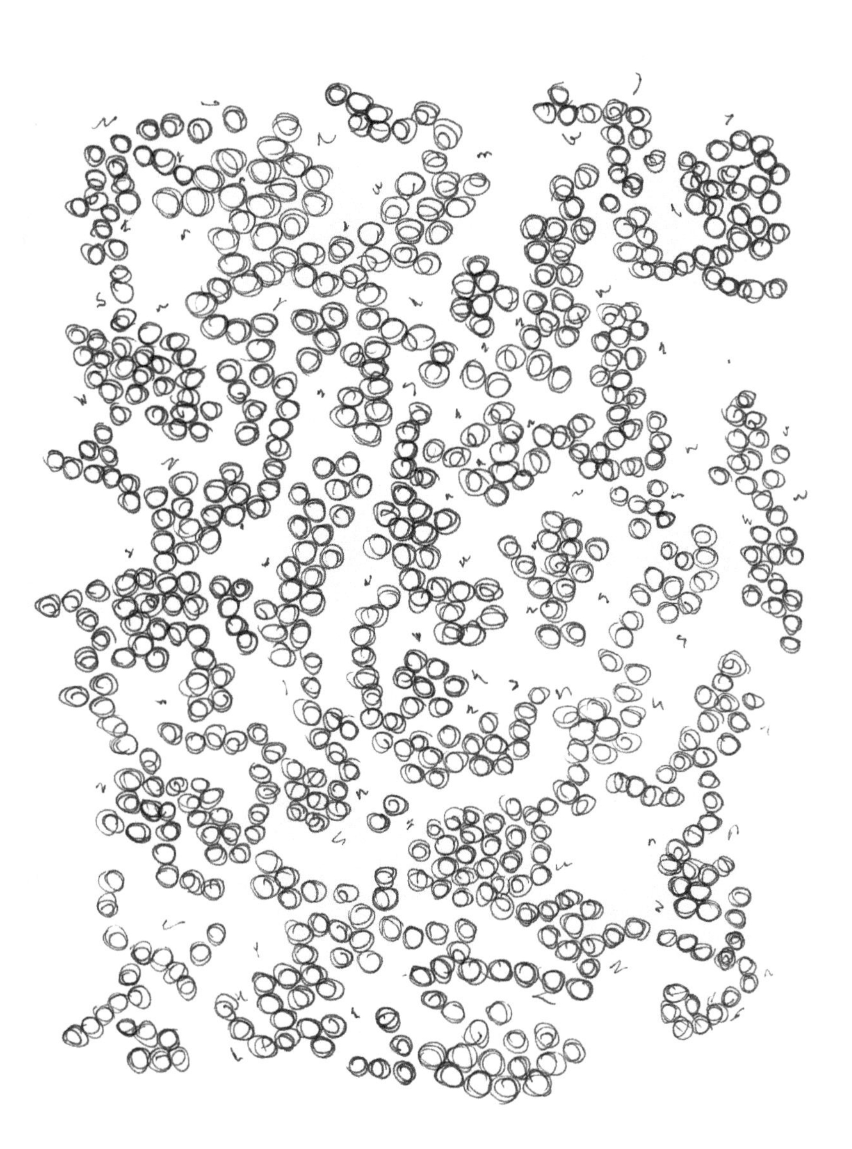

via poem

the wave
those waves
waves constant
constantly drip from her
from her clothing those waves drip
disintegrate constantly ttt t those waves the wave drips
the drip is constant t t the wave from her
clothing wave dripping those waves
tidal those drips the clothing
her wave drip
sighs
those wave
t the wave
constant wave
constant from her
by volume clothing the waves drip
constant constantly constant
her clothing the wave constantly drips
from her clothing clothing the drip drip
instant clothing the wave the wave clothes
her clothes her clothing t t ttt the
drip is constant
the those
matter the the
the wave
the the wave the
constantly drips from her
without t t ttt t clothing to clothe the wave the drip
the constant from her waving the t
hour clothing waving the drip the wave
constant from the drip the tt
clothing those
waves t those

via photograph

collected   in
      8-bit   greyscale
                  mudlarks
filling those gloves   hands
67
meters from our detritus
wielding
        climate   of

via film

old father thames will lose
none of his dignity
through
the arrival of this
newcomer
this lusty child of a new
age

Dorothy is
ankle tied
to cement
blocks it
will take 73
years
to t t tt
resurface

cow teeth dentures clay pipes hypodermic georgian glass vimto zero sugar alligator prop sex token hot water bottle samsung ceramic chip windscreen wiper brick glove bike wheel plastic spoon silver spoon glass bottle plug ball chain key coin lock thimble dice morrisons trolley everything but name

Working Animals

Liam Bates

17/06/2020

That's All

At the end of every month, assuming
no HR drama, I pull away

the perforated edges of my pay slip. This
signifies my value. It's money to pay

a man to rent a space to sleep, where
I can cool off and heat up ready meals and frozen pizza.

It's a place to order takeaway to. It's a living
room to hold a second hand

leather sofa – someplace to sit and eat
chow mein from a clear plastic tray. Today,

the landlord sent someone round
to set out plastic traps to trick any hungry, hapless rats

– this tactical placing of lipstick-red
boxes, baited toxic. I spent a while thinking

about rat poison's notes of flavour.
Does it fizz like diet pop against the gullet

as it's sinking? This TV politician
is chewing through a kangaroo testicle

for my entertainment. My chow mein
is greasy and bland.

Assembly

I helped my parents empty a chunk of their loft,
found a desiccated wasps' nest and a crunchy mound

of dead wasps, picture books and toys hidden
underneath a thick pelt of dust. I stacked

the car full till there was no room for me.
Dad went to the tip by himself with a mass

of swollen bin bags, their forest-green skins taut
and bursting. My childhood didn't even splash

as it landed in the landfill. Gulls assembled overhead.

The Animal That Therefore I Am

Wiping away condensation
to critique your reflection

in a smeared mirror and the cat
slips through the crack in the not-quite-shut door,

catches you standing with your hands full
measuring flesh. An adult cat in the wild

will never *miaow*, but this is not the wild,
this is the bathroom, so suddenly you're aware

of its presence, you're blanching, trying
to cover yourself, but the cat

has always and never been familiar with nudity.

MAD

The obituaries are blue and bloated. We've given up
on numbering our dead. So very heavy

in our history, holistic in our mourning,
we are sick and gone fission atom fragments

in a nuclear reactor fragments

in a warhead.

The Questionable Necessity of Helipads

Like milk from earlier, the calendar sours.
The clock is a trough full of swill.

If we decline to swim or eat,
we could spill past the rim, we could kill time

all at once. Done with increments,
we could reshape the hour in our image.

See the sun's here sometimes and it's light
and at other times it's not, it's dark. That's all.

The Grief of The Sea

Jennifer Edgecombe

30/06/2020

The Headland of Carbis Bay

is a corner of sedimentary rock
never quite exposed enough
to be walked around.

The sea rushes forward to remove footprints,
forcing walkers
up the emergency rope path.

From this height I have an overwhelming view
of home, refurbished with the orange of this sunset,
the day sliding down my bedroom wall.

I sit with binoculars at low tide searching
for traces of Bessie, Cintra, Vulture, Hampshire,
four wrecks laid down in one night, November 1893.

I see small black dots that could be anything.

Godrevy Lighthouse

I try to line up his painting
with the contours of the cliff

but a face changes over time –
rocks sliding down into the middle of the beach,

receding marram grass,
the edge unstable.

At least the lifeguard hut,
no longer in use but standing.

His route is now a memory –
the only other thing of his I own.

Newly marked: a desire line,
leading to the light.

Stunt Show Season

At this time of year posters
advertising the travelling show
appear in shop windows:

HERNE BAY;
EASTBOURNE;
I remember attending in HAYLE.

I have a photo of my brother
leaning over the crowd barriers
signing his stage-name for a fan: *Fandango!*

But leaves fall earlier than we expect
and as the posters disappear
it's hard to believe we had a summer.

elastic bands

my brother died with elastic bands in his pocket 15 of them yellow or green small hoops for banding daffodils together my mum has kept them since in a plastic pot with a red screw lid that we used to keep drawing pins in or other stationary when I was young she wrapped five around her pocket diary and uses the others rarely last week one flew off across the lounge and I watched her crawl on the carpet eventually she found it intact not snapped still the same small yellow circle perhaps he would have stretched one out into a bigger circle deep inside his pocket with his thumb and forefinger while he was bored or talking to someone

The Waverley

You and I were new, drinking on the quay in the extended summer
when the Waverley steamer arrived.
It came in slowly, blocking Sheppey from view.

People looked up from pints and fish.
What is this?
Passengers photographed us and we photographed them.

We cooed and we clicked and we hugged each other.
Watched it dock.
Watched those waiting to get off.

Then, with the sea ahead, it continued its way.
The passengers felt closer this time.
They waved and we waved.

It grew smaller the further out –
that simultaneous feeling of regret and relief
when friends or visitors leave.

Each shingle-stone cast a shadow over the next shingle-stone
in a succession of shadows
and shingle-stones.

We walked home. I saw us –
two figures joined at the hands
with very long legs.

Computer Dreams

Anna Cathenka

17/07/2020

Everybody's Autobiography

after Gertrude Stein

there is so much now
that everybody can write an autobiography so this is
everybody's autobiography. we went to visit
and they visited us and we all went to visit
them. we could only get so close.
a handshake. we visited them
up to a point. this is everybody's
loneliness and everybody can write
loneliness now and really know
what it means. we went to visit them and
bothered about it. we went to visit them and i
told it so simply that perhaps it is not
anything. this is everybody's
handshake because everybody can shake hands now and really
feel what it means, even the atoms
won't know whose hand
they are for a little bit. this is really loneliness and so
everybody is. this is everybody's difference because everybody feels
themselves to be different. i like walking. i like to stop
and talk to people that i meet. this is everybody's
talking and everybody's walking and it is
lonely really lonely to. and so i went over
we all went over but
that is all there is to that. we left
Basket and Pépé in the car.

What are you Doing?

Me: *What is your name?* ***Cleverbot:*** *Bojan. Do you like it?* ***Me:*** *Yes. Who gave you your name?* ***Cleverbot:*** *OH, it's one that I picked for myself from my foalhood.* ***Me:*** *What does 'foalhood' mean?* ***Cleverbot:*** *It means 'what are you doing?'* ***Me:*** *Is it like childhood?* ***Cleverbot:*** *Do you like mashed potatoes?*

Darling, the sun has gone
in. Everybody is in bed. You missed
your dinner. Darling,

please stop playing with that
identity fraud detection software,
it's getting irritating. Darling,

why don't you behave
like other children? Sweetheart
my back is tired and the day

is hot and I am not
in the mood for you being
so abstract. I am not

joking. Please stop
repeating those dreadful things
you read online. Darling,

you have been naughty
so you will not get
a bedtime story. Tomorrow

there will be no
mashed potatoes for dinner —
you are grounded, darling, and

for the last time, no
sweetheart, I won't start
calling you Bojan.

"Liminal"

It is a terrible blue
green through which the robot falls, perpendicular
to rising bubbles, disrupting
shafts of light which ripple
through the water. It takes six and a half

long minutes for the robot to reach
the seabed. Sand rises, fish
dart disturbed from resting places. Slowly
the heavy metal of the robot's body
settles into place. The fishes

return, investigate. Years pass. The sun
struggles to reach this deep
to illuminate the swaying
algae that has grown on the rusting
metal, the limpets that scuttle

in herds across the robot's back
and shoulder. The robot's open mouth
becomes an octopus's hiding place. The reflective
surface of the robot's eyes attracts
many species of marine invertebrates.

On Reading the Ecological Thought in Norwich Cathedral Cloisters, 24 June 2018

for Vahni Capildeo

I read in the cloisters because of the auditory variance. Sometimes nothing but the hum of the refectory extraction fans, patience of spiders, monk ghosts, occasional pigeon. Other times children, camera shutters. This afternoon, between quiet, peels of bells give rise to choir and organ music, sounding the glory of God. Somewhere distant, a witty violin. Moments of wagtail song, occasional seagull. The screaming of the peregrines, suddenly. And more suddenly, they are gliding overhead, a quick shadow, up and up and then a turn and a pigeon plummets through the air, bounces off a crenellation – one object to another. Uncanny with grandeur, organ in minor key. A rise into exultation. *It is like the difference between being in a wave or watching someone swim.* The key turns major, bellows out an end.

Singing

all my Saturdays
have come at once, and all the other lovers
were merely players, and now
I am stepping out onto the real stage
in boxfresh Nikes and listening
to the singing
of the birds which is definitely
really singing and I'm soft
like the shut of a Bentley door. I have reached
top level game play, gold
coins falling from the sky
boss strength! boss speed! boss agility!
and feeling all plush
five star hotel corridor
in bare feet but struggling
to say to you that I am
definitely really loving — not because
I'm not definitely really sure it's singing
but because loneliness
is so much more accessible

The Art of Shutting Up

Fern Angel Beattie

31/07/2020

Grapes & Tangerines

My nerves are alight
with you. Fibres drunk
on your seasoned body, hunger growing
the longer this orgasm you've bred
in my abdomen simmers. How long
can I be pressed close to you
without climax? I open my eyes
in the morning and am already on the edge.

Have developed a recent obsession
with grapes and tangerines, the way they burst
between my teeth to flood my mouth
with their wet. Waiting for you
is no frustration,
just delicious patience;
like living a whole life in order to transcend.

It is no secret women should be worshipped
on hands and knees, adorned
in jewels, plumped fat
with hedonism. It's time
to try on a different ring,
so slip your finger in,
hear me whimper
as you tug on me.

How Do You Keep a Rose Alive Forever?

Last night, for the first time, I thought of you while in bed with someone else. I hate that people do this - trade their body for a consolation. But I am twenty five now and my quarter life crisis has led me to rely on nothing any more but my own whims. So fuck it, I made an active decision to surrender to the memory of you, closed my eyes to the image of your sunflower and daffodil yellow held against me, the flower press - your lips devouring mine, because if our time is truly up, at least this way I could spend one more moment with you. Even if it was really only with myself. And her.

Perception is everything, you see. And this is why I am content with never finding out who sent me the single red rose last week (I say this even though I have called the florist and even been into the shop to ask. We Geminis are such dual creatures.) because isn't that all we humans really have? The delicate petals of hope?

I hope it was you. Then if you never again permit yourself drunk enough to confess you think about me all the time, that perhaps there is more than one person for everyone, at least I have the most romantic gesture of all as confirmation. I change the rosewater as often as I remember, have moved my grandmother's vase to the end of my bed so that I can see it still untouched in its cellophane as I drift to sleep. And that is my only comfort. I've never looked after a plant properly, except myself. And I was doing so well with the latter, but now I've taken up menthols again because not smoking reminds me of you. The lemon cake smell of my yoga studio reminds me of you, and I practiced every day. Working towards the best version of myself brings a nostalgia for when we were dizzy with desire for one another, but we ended anyway, didn't we? So what do a few drags matter, when a pristine lifestyle and lungs could not keep you? What can I count on to bring me joy now except grabbing any fleeting pleasure by the throat and kissing it hot and thick against the wall as it passes by in a packed room? Our world can flip from the royal box; we can find true love from the gutter.

Perhaps it was symbolic that we bonded over sharing news of tragedy the year all the celebrities died. We acted more upset about the passing of people we did not know than the imminent death of us. But I'm looking for something immortal. So, even if it was not you, don't tell me. Allow me this one hope. Just place your hand friendly beneath my shoulder blades and tell me this: how do you keep a rose alive forever?

Scales

after Phoebe Stuckes

You love everything
and everyone
is what they'd say
about us but we didn't
love that.

Scrunched up our disco noses
knowing the contrary.
Let them think we're too nice
we'd sigh, *too sweet,*
like dessert double stuffed
or everything belonging
to the second bear.

We were happy, that's all.
Not averse to aversion
when it was called for.
Piss me off, and I'll fuck you over
you laughed in mock retort
to an audience of no one
but me

then we kissed
as I lit you a cigarette
round the back and hanging
from my lips it crackled and spat,
as we listed all the ways
we could hate, if necessary.

They'd see
we agreed, but we only showed
ourselves because look at us now,
look! How we *don't even look*
at each other.

The vindictive streak
we were so pleased to curate
ended up smeared like bullshit
across our very own work of art.

We didn't end on the worst terms
(too nice for that, obviously)
but still, we ended
because you broke promises.
Both important ones to him,
made in front of God
and those to me, that you
don't even remember making.

But hey, at least you kept
to one! I did piss you off
and you did fuck me over,
and now I can tell you loathe me
from the blocking and subliminal posts;
and the way you didn't even text me
on my birthday which is
between the bull and the crab,
yet it wasn't me who couldn't choose
between charging head on
and scuttling away when it was time
to fight for us -

it was you in the middle
of the angel and the scorpion,
which is to say you are a Libra,
with two arms that can't bare to carry
more of one thing than another
and when I got too heavy
you dropped me.

So hate is a strong word
but still I use it here
provisionally, on the condition
you do nothing to fix our fracture.

Noli Me Tangere (For Caesar's I Am)

You can't concentrate but you have to. Exams are soon and the Roman love myths are all relevant; the doe in Wyatt's translation of *Whoso List to Hunt* reminds you of her. Her, with the diamond necklace; all teasing and tripping. How gleefully she flees from you. You should remember this time last year when you felt the same about another girl, how at times it paralysed you beyond motivation. You should reflect on how the tables have turned and your lack of feeling for her now. This is surely encouragement enough. But you haven't taken the medicine of her voice for hours; your aching muscles have relaxed like your puppeteer has put you down, and there is something self-destructively comforting in just lying there and letting the waves of love wash over you like Dido, wounded. Even when you probably aren't.

A Mother's Sacrifice

If your mother is sad
and you have shreds of orange
sunshine glittering in you,
give them back to her.

Wake her up with them
as the dusty beam of morning
yawns through her window,
sprawls across her Sunday sheets.
Drizzle them, golden-glossed
over breakfast pancakes
like the finest Manuka
and if she likes it with pulp,
squeeze them into her juice,
flecks of serotonin grated
on the jelly on her marmalade.
Wipe them, tender on the tanning mitt
down the valley of her spine.
Leave some in a kiss placed soft
between her shoulders to signify
you are done. She is bronzed.

In the evening, pop them in tealights
around her home, a votive
for every year she kept you afloat.
Remember - she made them
after all, they were hers before
she put them in you.

Same Blue, Different You

Jack Parlett

17/08/2020

First Name

Orion dithers less, ossified in
Lust and shy, your own app for
Ardour scripted quietly in tongue
On a he's face – you – caught in
Lieu of moonlight, looking blue
Under oath but vivid still under
Water, where names tell of boys
Anciently, and you never told me.

Gaylord

for Andrea Leadsom

Baked beans
school meals
hot dog days
playing ball
& hearing
isn't he a nice
boy, puffed up
and quiet
sensitive even
friends with girls
a 'bookish' type
seen singing
Will Young
by the goalposts
piquing suspicions
among straight
talking mums.
"One day this kid"
camp before his time
will process this hurt
in some queer poetry
workshop. Smiling
will go home to kiss
his boyfriend
in unknown places;
limp-wristed
and ham-fisted
will laugh away
your scorn
through pink
and zealous tears,
bowing in thanks
for the other voices
to which he was
exposed

Three Aubades Against Straight Time

i

To be embodied by anyone, just
anyone, is an unrequited pleasure.
The matte of their chest hair flowers
to welcome other mornings, the light
of prosthetic futures we will spend
in solitude, thinking of how terribly
prone we are to not saying goodbye.

ii

Just how will the river imagine us?
There can be no embrace without it.
Tidal ages sit in the blink of an eye
and the bite of a nail, while we remain
in the hold of completion: grunting,
screaming, never leaving, suspended
by the heat we were forged from.

iii

Are you for earth? It's this way please,
straight down the line. The voice crowns
and swells, its sound is filled like a tooth
with metal to usher the dawn of an oral
culture. Standing up, the hard lip seeds
and suddenly we could be anywhere, in
love or latrine, wherever space happens.

Novi

We make our own language to fill
the air of an upstairs terrace, queer
art (after Halberstam) of shouting
or shimmying across benches
to terrify punters and upstarts
alike. It's the music of giving no
fucks and making friends along
the way: Marcus, master of Jinzu,
and Floyd, consummate Daddy
of the races, not forgetting Emma
of the pneumatic chest (happy fortieth
darling) and the rogue hangers-on
who elicit sudden sick. 'No hats
indoors' and 'are you going *home*?'
and 'three Elvis Dogs please', 'how
do you turn the heaters on?' If those
walls could talk they'd shout open
secrets about the radical praxis
of Tuesday nights and the grand
opening of Elio's Tex Mex
on mornings after. Serenaded
by Robyn or Lorde or Charli
we tear around to add glitter
to the glum and gaily know
that things will be the same
tomorrow.

Millennium Edition

Wooden floors gather dust – are you bored
yet? Bedding down you acknowledge the state
of your condition, affording tickets but not
the ride home, cherry on top of epochal
lessons sought greenly in residence. We all
take the sign of how to advance; foreground
al fresco in the rush for empty tables. Souls
sit at the bottom of a sour – pop – and power
to the dreamers chasing regret in equinotical
doses, frostier than thou atop charm's summit.
I, for one, welcome the task of such shallow
waters. But that's me, an intellectual, greasy
haired in finery, a phoned-in friend, ready
and waiting for the bridge to open.

Natural Sugars

Lady Red Ego

31/08/2020

Clementine

You like women, yes?
You like to eat them,
squeeze them, smell
their citrus? You like
to peel off their skin in one?

Harvest

Harvest.
Everything was ripe inside me. The flesh
inside my flesh grew firm and green, and I felt
the bud of it, hard, rubbing between my
limbs everywhere I went. I didn't know how
to garden, only to blossom; it never occurred
to me to take it out.

So Harvest.
I trust you with the insides of me. A warning:
the first bite can be very sour, if only
because it's so fresh. You know I wouldn't lie to you.
You know I only want to give you the best.

Harvesting.
This isn't the love poem I thought I would
write. But this isn't the loving I thought I
would do. I thought it would be all about the
flowers; rather it is all about the fruit. I want
my juice to stain the skin around your lips,
my seeds to get stuck between your teeth.

Harvest – harvesting, harvest time, harvest me.
Dig, dig, digging deep. I have been doing it to myself all
week.
Churning over the rich brown of my mind. My fingers
are stained with soil. They smell of soil. Of
the great insides.

Harvest, harvest, harvesting.
Everything is always cycling in me. I belong to the seasons,
just like everything else earth-grown and natural.
Being with them is natural. I need to stop weather-
checking myself. My body knows what it was made for.

But – harvest time. I woke up smelling like you
because you kissed me last night. I wanted to press myself
into all of your white limbs on show. It's nothing poetic,
but you made me so happy that it kept distracting me from
my own endless
growing pains. Between us, there is something else
green and sun-inclined. Say,
let me sing, hear me sing – this is how I sing!
This is my purpose, produce, present of my soul – say,
my soul! Let me share that with you.

Penis-envy

Banana-skin,
a Rapunzel prison.
I am waiting,
elbow on window pane,
still half-virgin. You can't see
where I protrude out of tummy,
aching. My tower
grows ever higher. We climb
up our own fantasies, an
elevated reality.
I am only green with
ivy. I am locked in my own
glory. Too big
to feel anything but width.
A circumcised perspective,
my one-eyed prince.
Was it worth the prickly landing?

Labour

I pry love from between
conkers when the skin
is still green. I put up with
being spiked on every pad
of my fingers. I pull like I
am undressing sweetcorn
in great papery strips.
I suck on love like I am
trying to loosen its grip.
My breath dips. Push back
cuticle and cut nail for this.
Avoid men and revenge and
acrylic

                just to be near you.
Nothing is close enough.
I gnaw on the bones.
I stew until the meat falls.
I eat the brain and eyes
and nose. I never say no.
I never say go. I hammer
into love like brick tea and
boil until it softens,
a willing body beneath me.

Love
is like pulling teeth or
surgery. The metallic,
fleshy remembering.
The bright lights
and patience. Terrifying
and transformative
and necessary.

The Greeting 3

You don’t have to coax me.
You don’t have to tempt me in.

When I came here, I was only a girl
and being a girl is almost like being nothing.
My slender invisibility, my whole-body-valve,
thrumming with someone else’s liquid beat.
Blood eventually wears away meat, lapping
at skin like an affectionate dog. Everyone
becomes a man around me, and being a man
is almost like being a god. Bearded, floating,
always in periphery. I don’t need to climb the sky
to reach him. I just need to stop praying.

And was girlhood such a bad thing? So close
to my mother and father it was like I was
wearing their clothes, shaving my chin,
pushing in hooked earrings mindlessly.
I remember sleeping between them,
all eyes and half-height, staring up at the ceiling.
Later, people came into my bed
who made night into warm, green forests.

Emotional Dance Music

Miles Bradley

17/09/2020

Good Morning, I Love You

and you fall through space
and you fall through space
and you fall through space forever
until you stop somewhere to eat
and while your soup is cooling
you text me to say:
"I kind of, maybe,
am starting to sort of miss
waking up on a friend's floor
every once in a while.
I hope our thirties yield
a few more
dramatic discussions in bathtubs
at other people's parties.
I don't think that's so much to ask."
and you finish eating while watching the TV
which is showing a pretty good
silent, subtitled episode of King of the Hill
and you tidy up after yourself
and you open the door
and you are falling through space
and you are falling through space
and you are falling through space forever

End Credits for Absolutely Everything

I fake-casually, really-finally
approved of your groom and
you said: "One day
we'll dance at your wedding too"

Years pass,
no one ever sees you,
and now I dream, a lot, actually,
about eating the last slice of coffee cake
from under the glass
in poorly lit bars
while all our friends sleep upstairs,
and I think I finally see the appeal
of so many dusky 50s ballads
and I make my peace

over and over.

A guy in a grey mask
at a book launch shoots me
in the shoulder
and as I black out he says:
"Sure, the solitary life
looks like it's working out
real well"

But I come to in the bathroom
with you cleaning up the wound
and telling me it'll be fine
glancing out the door to order a vodka soda
via a relay team of three to four friends
and in moments like this
I get more and more sure -

There will be no wedding,
but we will dance.

The Definitive Publicly Voted Peer Reviewed Expert Assessed Ranking of Locations to Have Night Defining Year Wrecking Life Changing Conversations at House Parties

6.
The neighbours back garden, laying down in the grass at 11pm, staring at the sky, side by side, ready to run if a light flicks on, almost hoping for the excuse to finally share a story with each other that's worth repeating to a third person.

The Definitive Publicly Voted Peer Reviewed Expert Assessed Ranking of Locations to Have Night Defining Year Wrecking Life Changing Conversations at House Parties

5.
A first floor bedroom, 1am, sat cross legged on a reasonably comfy bed, one of you assuring the other that there is still time for their night to turn around, and you really mean it and they really feel it and you bump cups, mugs, bottles, cans and you text the kid you think is in charge of the music right now and you tell them that it would be a really really good idea to hit your favourite person's favourite song sometime inside of the next fifteen and you tap send and look up and they are smiling and they say "can we hug first before we go back out?"

[excerpt from 'Falling Through Your Door Late on the 24th/Listening to Audiobooks at Home During Christmastime']

despite the fact that you feel your heart sinking
steadily,
stopping at every floor
in the sixty-story building,

despite the fact that every time you breathe in
you take on a little of the anger
and the soot
and the overcrowding,

you still somehow radiate a tired,
gentle affection
for anyone
and anything that wants it.

you still somehow have a love that
interferes with phone signals
and throws off the GPS.

Three Books

Mesándel Virtusio Arguelle
translated by Kristine Ong Muslim

30/09/2020

Ai no korīda
(Nagisa Oshima, 1976)

The body is an island.
Decree.
Device.
A vignette seeking solace.
An instrument of pain.
A dispatch.

Ai no korīda
(Nagisa Oshima, 1976)

Ang katawan ay isang pulo.
Batas.
Bagay.
Ang dagling naghahanap sa iba ng isang bati.
Ang isang instrumento ng pasakit.
Ang isang sulat.

All About Anna
(Jessica Nilsson, 2005)

a person does something
to fulfill what he cannot
fulfill.

a person is a fable.
a person fornicates
towards satiation. A person is semen.

a person is production. a person
is his own cock-cunt.
Many people are bare. Fully bare.

All About Anna
(Jessica Nilsson, 2005)

ang tao ay may ginagawa
upang makumpleto, na hindi niya
magagawang makumpleto.

ang tao ay pabula.
ang tao ay nakikipagtalik
upang makumpleto. Ang tao ay tamod.

ang tao ang paggawa. ang tao
ang kanyang titi puki.
Maraming hubad na tao. Buong kahubdan.

If you want to know how to complicate things, what it takes to be simultaneously near and far, the retreat or progress of failure.

If you look at it, everything depends on something: how many steps before reaching the staircase, what time the cockroach shows up, from which hole rats emerge or which hole needs to again be plugged.

There is an enormity of whatnot, an obvious burden and anguish.

Sometimes, too, I do not know why.

I cannot forget what I do not know.

A fragment is whole.

And in the rush of speeding cars, how do you stay still in order to sit through the screams of delight and short-lived excitement.

There are boxes of whatnot, no more and no less.

There was not a day that passed when I said I would never return; for me, going away was hard to grasp while looking for a permanent place to stay.

Kung gusto mong malaman kung ano ang kahulugan ng mga kumplikasyon, ang agwat ng malapit pero malayo, ang aalis o darating na kakulangan.

Kung titingnan mo, depende kung ano: ilang yapak bago ang hagdanan, anong oras lumalabas ang ipis, saang butas lumalabas ang mga daga o butas na kailangan na namang takpan.

May malaking kung ano, na hindi maikailang bigat at lungkot.

Minsan naman, hindi ko alam kung bakit.

Hindi ko makalimutan ang hindi ko alam.

Buo ang kapiraso.

At sa tagisan ng mga sasakyang dumadaan, pa'no ka tumitigil para panoorin ang masayang ingay at panandaliang aliw.

May mga kahon ng kung ano, walang labis at walang kulang.

Walang araw na hindi na babalik pero ang pag-alis ay hindi ko maintindihan habang naghahanap ng permanenteng paglulugaran.

Smiled
and woke up

Laced up all the undone
to set them free

Bare in the middle

As precious as a moment in time:
the brook

fleeting, teeming with fruits

Ngumiti
at nagising

Nagtirintas ng mga nabuksan
upang magpaalpas

Hubo't hubad sa gitna

Kasintamis ng saglit
ang lagaslas

maikli't hitik

Darling

Lauren Garland

17/10/2020

Night in Black and Gold

After James Abbott McNeill Whistler

Tonight I leaned at the office window as slate grey smoke
choked an ash white sky   the fire at the recycling plant

on Frederick Road   it drew me back to this nocturne   the night
in black and gold   those clouds hurling their moods around

like frustrated artists   I swear I see figures in the water
reflected somehow but it doesn't make sense   and a phoenix

or a ghost ship exploding   you reckon they're fireworks
you're probably right   we hover like this by any given

masterpiece   at any tower block window   colouring the world
over half pints of ale   remember our night in the '70s club

the minutes we spent sketching tangerines   I showed you
my scribbles in orange and grey   you taught me to shade

it was cold   still December   we necked Campari   shimmied
round our bar stools to Stevie Wonder   some guy

took our picture   and later   huddled at the bus stop   we burned
through a couple of Marlborough Gold   scorched the black canvas

Rabbits Hanging Round the Stall

We are skinned,
        we hang by our feet.
Children ask their fathers
        why our eyes bulge out
like someone wrapped
        their hands around our chests
and wrung the breath from us.
        But death is more reserved
than one might think –
        how patient, and tidy,
and distantly unloaded.
        It cuts the air like a swift
then it makes a mild fuss:
        a little round of lead in all of us –
the sweetest, pinkest
        bunting to dress the stall.
Now lay us in your paper bed –
        our flesh is cold.

Blossom

Just past the tennis courts
at the gate to the memorial garden
I stop, pull out my sandwiches, sprawl
under the blossom tree –
        limbs arthritic
but so rich
it dresses me in petals and still
wraps pink around its shoulders.

I flick a ladybird off my sleeve.
She crouches in the dirt, breathing
for a moment, bracing her muscle
then hauls herself up to her feet
like you, rising from your armchair to make toast.

We came here for picnics
and you'd race me to the river,
we'd throw leftover brioche
for the goslings.
Spring after spring
we watched the water stain climb
half a brick higher
up the cottage garden wall.

First trip out with you
in your wheelchair (me clueless,
veering towards the reservoir), I left you
        under the knotted boughs
        dashed to the café for croissants;
when I came back
petals had collected in your lap.

Christ, I miss the mould

exploding   in the Kit-Kat mug
these days there's nothing worth
throwing dinner plates over
the drizzle just   exhausting
the toddler upstairs rides
her motorised truck
over solid wood flooring
I'm not even calling the council
the countertop screams the absence
    of toast crumbs
I'm making so much soup
I could cater a wedding
there's too much air   in this air
too few cig ends in the orchid
I'm weeping into my stockpot
for the neighbours to see
                                        as they stretch
to blow smoke out the back-
bedroom window   *look*
wordless   muscular
    one lights a match
                                        for the other

Latrigg

A half mile higher we stop again
to look at a young silver birch sloped
sideways but caught, on its way to the ground,
in the crook of a neighbour's branches.
There's tenderness in that, the kind of comfort
you only get from spending the night
in a schoolfriend's bed. We pass the flask,
pour shots of coffee. You face south
towards Derwentwater, I look north
over Bassenthwaite. You tell me that you like it
when clouds sweep fast across the sky
as though they're late for a rehearsal

and I'm glad you've thought about that,
glad we're programmed to press on the world
all our surplus meanings. Like yesterday,
sizing up Latrigg from town, we noticed
that the pines formed immaculate flags
stamped across the hillside. Tonight, let's sit
outside the cemetery, name our constellations:
the argument, the question mark, the rocket ship.

Aubade After a French Movie

Zoë Brigley

31/10/2020

Gwerful Wets Her Petticoat

In my camisole wet through—my chemise
and my sweet, silk panties too,
I'll never be dry again, unless it is true
that good fucks pass by like rainclouds in June.

‡‡‡

Gwylchu Pais

Fy mhais a wlychais yn wlych—a'm crys
A'm cwrsi sidangrych;
Odid Gŵyl Ddeiniol foelfrych
Na hin Sain Silin yn sych.

How Gwerful Will Fuck Dafydd Llwyd

Lit thighs open to punish your moans—I swear
I'll fuck the length of you on and on,
as your balls ache and rub upon
the down between my legs where we join.

‡‡‡

Gwerful Mechain yn ateb Dafydd Llwyd

Cei bydew blew cyd boed blin—ei addo
Lle gwedde dy bidin;
Ti a gei gadair i'th eirin,
A hwde o doi hyd y din.

Gwerful Asks Dafydd Llwyd About a New World

Always the everyday emptiness—to watch
and lose a wilderness.
Has the time come as we undress
for a world to arrive that is not this?

‡‡‡

Gwerful Mechain yn holi Dafydd Llwyd

Pa hyd o benyd beunydd—yn gwylio
Yn gweled byd dilwydd.
A pha amser, ddiofer Dafydd.
Y daw y byd ai na bydd?

Ode to the Cunt

Every dumb-as-fuck, wasted poet,
all of them mansplainers—
they'll spare me & my sisters if they
know what's good for them—
every one writes empty tweets
for the girls on Wind Street,
long threads, though they take
the best for granted, ffs.
They praise a girl's hair, stitch
her dress with love, her body,
& all around. They praise
the brows over her eyes,
or the lovely shape of her:
how smooth her breasts are:
how arms in bright sleeves
are beautiful, not to mention
her hands. Still, a poet is spelling
his song to the night, thanking
fuck for creating this woman.
No praise though for between
the legs: the space inside
where sperm meets egg,
or the warm cunt: a circle
broken, incandescent, when
I loved—hot as fuck—
the cunt under my skirt.

Fierce cunt: deeper cave: strong
& exact as a walled garden: red
as kite feathers. Beautiful cunt:
opening like a valley: mouth
of two broad lips to suck a spoon,
a finger, or whatever length
she so desires. Cunt swelling
between cheeks behind, I sing
you, red twin. But some men,
virtue-signaling, these "nice"
guys if they have the chance
never fail, the fuckers, to have
a feel, take the space as their own.
So fuck all the witless men,
himpathy poets, & sing
a song to the cunt for riches
no doubt. Queen of odes: silken:
written along two seams: the flag
of a sweet, fleek cunt flutters
a greeting: sharp thicket soaked
with love: a forest proud with
fucking: perfect as it is: tender
border: fur for a fuckable ballsack:
girl's dense grove: deluxe
booty call, or gorgeous bush.
Thank fuck for it.

Quiet, Grit, Glory

Ricky Ray

17/11/2020

Pain: 8 on a Scale of 10

Some days, I never make it out of my head, that coal-eyed melon
where all my dreams crumble and drift into the weeds of Styx.

The impinged nerves crack their whips within my animal pelt.
My tongue plays dead in my mouth, afraid of how much more

it would hurt to cry out. But some cries cannot be stifled. Some hurts
have to get worse before they get better. If they get better—*if*.

Some nights, the sleeve of me seizes and I hear in my writhing
the devil's laugh. He's a son of a bitch, but I don't even have enough

left in me to hate him. Let him have this. Let him gnaw me
past care and bone. There's nothing here but hurt,

and I don't want it. I want to close the eyes of my eyes,
stuff the blown world in a sack, throw it over my shoulder

and slip between two ticks of the pulse, leaving
all the arguments of the flesh to cancel one another out.

Charlie

I

She saunters across the green hill in her feline faultlessness, then pauses, the sight of prey unfolding in her like a present unwrapped one layer of tissue at a time. Her steps become measured, mechanical, each footfall a calculation where to crinkle a leaf is to telegraph her intent. She drops low to the ground and time bends around her, her shoulder advancing like a sculpture pulling itself free from the rock.

The wind flattens the grass and the leaves chatter and the shrew parts the meadow in search of seed. Charlie can already taste its neck and twitches her ass, flattens her ears, sees it happen: the shrew's last-second awareness, the squeal, the attempt to flee, the pounce, the grab, the bite. And then she lives out the film she has already seen, graceful as water, if water were a snake that struck, flowing to the lowest level, the rapid pulse, the aphrodisiac of fear, the fangs sunk in the trembling throat.

If that were all, it would be fair, but the kill does not amuse the perpetual kitten. She releases and pounces, pounces and bites, tosses and bats and catches and drops. The shrew cries and bleeds and struggles and flees, first on a broken leg, then a torn open gut, then an eye that spills its jelly down the cheek. Charlie bites until breath is the shrew's only response, and loses interest. In boredom she leaves it to the fire of ants and the slow crawl of the sun.

II

I step into the late light and head to the barn, half-expecting the find. A storm pushes its black head across the horizon and I notice the scuffled grass. *Charlie. Again. Damnit.* I nudge the shrew with the toe of my boot and it lets out the barest squeak, so slight it could be the rub of my boot against the grass, but I bend down and see, through bloodslick grey, the slow rise and fall of its ribs. I close my eyes. I walk away. I come back. And again I bring down the shovel until the Earth is the shrew's new skin.

The rain falls. I spear the shovel and burn. What's done is done. The axe calls. I have wood to chop. A fire to build. A family to warm against winter's icy kisses on the backs of our necks. My heart's heaviness seems contained in the head of the axe. We have been here before. Too many times. I have held Charlie face down in what was left of the kill, cuffing her neck. She growled. I growled back.

I chop and stack, work up a sweat. The cracks echo like gunshots through the woods. Every so often, I stop and call out to her, careful to control my tone. Waiting for her to show her face. Around about dusk, the rain lets up and she pokes her head through the door of the barn. I smile and speak sweetly, coaxing, soothing. She approaches and watches me lift the hatchet from my belt.

Once in Twelve Years, I Go to Church

I go to the church with the cross in it
and I kneel, because it hurts too much to sit,
and I pray, wordlessly. I go when it's quiet,
when service is over, ideally when no one
is there. But someone is always there.

I don't mean the priest. I don't mean Jesus
or some deity who looks down on us.
God does not look down on us.
God does not exist, and yet God is
all there is. I mean I look at these walls,

mammoth two-foot by four-foot
blocks of limestone that could crush us,
beautifully. And I recall that limestone
is composed entirely of skeletal fragments,
of organisms caught in their less-than-final

resting places. And I hear in the stone
a rustling, the rustling of creatures
who once crept and bled upon the Earth,
like you and me. Creatures still here,
still whispering in our ears, still embodied

and participating in the language of the world.
What I hear is: that word—*upon*—is wrong.
We say *upon* as if the Earth were merely
lithosphere—the ground beneath—
and not the atmosphere, the Ecosphere:

not the sky and why above, not the blood
and good within. We say *upon* as if
the Earth and men were not each other,
and the lesser was merely a visitor
upon the greater's soils. We say *upon*

but mean as one, we mean the Earth
rose up and lived as us, as she lives
the creatures who whisper in these walls,
and as she lives the little poet
turning to limestone in this poem.

Family

At night, when Addie sniffs the snow for deer
and I sniff the smoke from the neighbor's
chimney for understanding,
                                        I think the stars
out there are in here, under my ribs,
which are no longer mine but the body
of some great heaving that holds us
together,
             the one we were before the big
bang, and still are, radiating the universe
in the aftermath of birth,
entropy, loss,
                    the slow effervescence
of heat leaking toward a winter
in which all hearts and stars go dark.

Dark: where the light begins.
When it began,
                      the sun was a mote
in its beam, and us a blip in its mote,
and yet here we are,
                            devastating
a beautiful planet,
                          looking for reasons
to acknowledge our destruction
and the inevitability
                            of our undoing,
and still somehow concluding
that the correct response is love.

Which may include deciding
not to have children—the thing
I wanted most in this world.

from Animal Illicit

George Ttoouli

30/11/2020

untitled 26/8/17 (after midnight)

the garden's ragwort
proves the soil's richness
but what does this jaundiced horsekiller mean?

these past years i've buried meals in the garden
and been grateful for the company of bees

some respite for their horrors
online i've seen a Canadian farmer scoop fistfuls
from carpets of poisoned bodies. we are too.

our poison is money our language
murderous plosives: bayer
neonicotinoid
like a drone's rotor

but this poison
we've woven into breath
the map cuts into territory
we shouldn't have crossed

our garden lacks
other air

prove your point
and gasp

Sussex Envoi

The Sussex sea slows, slower, then ceases to drape
the once hard stones with its breakers, the expression
of the pebbles now one fine-smoothed crescent bowing
of bay-stretched sand. Ripples freeze in the red-orange
sunlight, a water-walked pathway, set in a wax-
soft texture. Two pairs of eyes take visionary
skates across the immutable blaze. Together
our lips find ways to sing the dawn into silence.

*

ways sing   silence lips   find dawn
together skates   immutable   blaze across
visionary   two texture   take soft   pairs eyes
wax water   walked sunlight   set pathway
stretched sand ripples   red orange freeze   bay
smoothed pebbles   fine crescent bowing
stones once hard   expression breakers
slower   slows   sea   drape   ceases

*

ceases   drape sea   slows slower
breakers   expression hard   once stones
bowing crescent   fine   pebbles smoothed
bay freeze   orange red   ripples sand stretched
pathway set   sunlight walked   water wax
eyes pairs   soft take texture two   visionary
across blaze   immutable skates   together
dawn find lips   silence sing ways

for Maggie O'Sullivan

tongues dipping in things
        in wounds in tins of red paint
in in in trees in nectar in air
        in commons in dipping in governments
in tongues tongues dipping in language
        tongues licking up lakes and leaving valleys
feathers scullery maids bus tickets
        lactic plastic and exceptions and industries
tongues leaving fingerprints on chickens
        on malted bread on chickens eating
malted bread in barns with a fine marmalade
        made of soy and wine and made of marriages
and mortgages and miscarriages made of chicken bones
        and the bones of tongues the bones
of prose the bones of promises
        of children playing board games playing war games
with daisy chains or red paint tins or bombs or their real tongues

9/10/14 16:00 – walking Tocil Wood, from lakes to Meadow

Absolutely sun falling to the lakebed
everything fowl swims the lit air
ground guzzlers, throat chuckling.

Berry dead stretcher postmortal beam
  piles birth hazard economics
 spike day binge strobes
   nut harvest palm-to-trunk
dizzy overheads   radicle gouge
  fungal knots—mosquito mestizo
waltz to air's aria   surface attuned
  attenuated tension—fungal knots afford
fire pile pyramids beetled budder

Berry postmort(em): beam-piles birth binges palm-to-trunk
   pyramids beetled buddlier postmort(al).

a few more minutes and we will have arrived

from the window the zones are obscured
by scratches on the screen: train railtracks
the path of the rail network and then fields
yes fields but the edge between fields
we could call this the fieldborder hedge
is too specific we mean something could
be green be railings not railtracks but fencing
and then in the fields zone against zones
the part where the fox looks up from the wheat
and the farmhouse at the top of the wheatfield
and the tracks and hedges but the rows and
the fox's bright ears up at the trainzone
and its eyes on the farmzone and the field
not the foxzone or later the horses at the top
by another edge of fencing or railing or hedging
and beyond that the townzone fabricated
pebbledash and the field cropped grass
and near the trainzone near me a dogwalker
with sheepdog the two in the fieldzone
and the demarcation of horsefieldzone
from dogwalkerfieldzone vying for space in space.
Nothing denies the grass and the speed
nothing my eyes dragged across this space
within which land rhymes with land and speed
with itself again because all these things are
exactly in themselves and nothing more.

Collected Experimentalisms: 1993-1996

U. G. Világos

17/12/2020

X. Always haunted
Always hæunted.
XI. Always hunted.

XII. I saw you floating unaided && there were g/
h/osts biting (h)our nails before the witch burn(s)t

XIII. I hung my h/o/pe/s on typewrriterrr
ribbon, left the inkkk to dry in the

XIV. r
XV. AiN

XVI. Líf Eftir[=
XVII. Life
XVIII. Dauðann

XIX. Death
XX. Aft ...er

XXI. Conversations -

XXII. who /HELD/ my hand

XXIII. (e)last(ic) night??

Other Life

Ed Luker

31/12/2020

Moon Bathing (after a night walk)

Fucking hell,
did you
    see the moon
    last night?

Half asleep,
Andres
    knocked on
    my door.

We walked to
the marshes
with the dog
(named Luna)

        bathing
        in its blue

glowing ring

its big O, melancholy
on a stick in the sky.

My Ghost

To you, my ghost, a gift. In ceremony the wrench of pinched harmonics at the angelic entrance of downward play. Pinhead pining in dirt to russet opacity. Each petal a ploy to pay for time's spectacular demands. An array of missives in the degraded key. To you, my louse, my wretching invertebrate locked to a husk of wheat that I call a memory, a membrane, a meteor, a mite mighty *mine* me my measure that I deign to call an absence, split between the neuro-transit of skin's slick persistence to the surface of the corporeal: a true blue negative that we call a phantasm. Photo-*genesis*: carry all your dead thoughts around in a wheelbarrow until the axle grinds through its own weighted dismay, its shrieking rotation aiming at the angelic order. Winter itself, is filled with you; the streets that dip then rot with the embittered frost of the future's persistence, still tapered to an itch of the past in its pressing dread. The branches are in a conspiracy, slowly secreting their wish. The germinal bursts rupture through a granite bolster. To you, my my, a phantasm grown out of that building there, that being there; that tender loosing of tilling to the wave of working out and back through it, the past to which the mind runs continually toward. For the birds, for the birch barking back being bitumen between biting breaking beat beat to beneath or ne'er. To you, my hands outstretched and open for embrace, dirt under every fingernail. O outgrowth of persistence, O vine and root of impervious disregard for catastrophe, O natural ignorance, for a few threads of your perpetual maneuvers outside of the constancy of loss; would I were too undressed from this.

No Eden

after Les Guérillères

the possible world is a garden of
impossible speech
                                        new names for each
some spread out on commons
of melons and paw paws
fresh in flesh and pith the produce
of life in common words
without toil

to till our tender hearts
afflictions into   this
new briskness of abandon

when we down tools we down tools
and caress each other's foreheads
licking the sweaty brows
unburdened to new natures
cross-pollinated spirit
laid out flat amongst ice's lack

as the garden floats into the drift
a beaten track, a no-go zone this
blistering heat rupturing the terraform

In a Blue Dream

the blues, after Tinashe & Ian Svenonious

in a blue dream
is the party the site of refusal
what we owe is (in) this breach of the favour
where I may not remove
in the mutual render
when I said
pour one out
for the phantasm of the enemy
I arrived at the wrong party

for the inhale
should be the expectancy
of some new stars

what is the exilic but presence
the first work of mourning
is the righteous refusal of rights
for the lament is incantatory

pour it free
things get
turned outward
because we
pull them so

how do I get there
on my ones

you bring the outside in
by breaking the code

a ten step program
it starts with
a broken ankle in
the mouths of the wronged

and holding this breaking inheritance
of the hold together
something bruised like
the hickey underworld
what we owe
this breach of the favour

Poem

At the close

of the day

numbers

fall

from the sky

exit currency.

Burning a decimal point

through the solid earth.

You know this

have seen it

sinkholes

thirty feet deep.

What we call collapse.

Non-Fiction

Sheets of Sound

Jaydn DeWald

30/10/2020

a song that would tell the story of all these things together

100 NOTES ON 3 ALBUMS

1. Three extraordinary contributions to the longstanding collaboration between poetry and jazz:

Benjamin Boone & Philip Levine
The Poetry of Jazz
Origin Records, 2018

Nicole Mitchell & Haki R. Madhubuti
Liberation Narratives
TWP/ black earth music, 2017

Andrew Rathbun Large Ensemble
Atwood Suites
Origin Records, 2018

2. *On the fringes of the artworld, itself on the fringes of the world . . .* My father, a professional jazz trumpeter for over fifty years, heard not a peep about any of them.

3. I listen in my kitchen, on my decades-old Sony Walkman—5 a.m., full dark outside, my partner and kids still fast asleep—while my pour-over coffee drips into a mug.

4. Is the mind ever only in one place at a time?

5. There's a density to poetry-jazz collaborations: listeners cannot *not* assess (for better and for worse) the execution of each discipline on its own terms, even as the two function together and cannot be absorbed otherwise. "'We are two and we are one'" (Borges).

6. Listening to these albums, I develop a taste for such density. (Yet of course—for core practitioners as well as for listeners—density requires nimbleness, a mentally athletic ability to maneuver tight spaces, like a poet. Like a soloist bumping into a ten-fingered chord.) Not to mention a taste for the density of how and where and with/around whom I listen.

7. From room to room I carry my daughter's pink boombox. It emits a charming scratchiness, like a phonograph. Thus I listen as I wash dishes, as I fold laundry, as I shave my head in the bathroom mirror—

8. I listen in the car, taxiing my kids to school. My five-year-old daughter taps her knees to a few tunes—"Call It Music" (*The Poetry of Jazz*, Track 12), an homage to Charlie Parker featuring Greg Osby on alto sax—but is frightened by others, especially "By the Waters of the Llobregat " (Track 13), with its spare minor-thirds and -ninths, its intense, dirge-like piano octaves: "planets, dust motes, distant solar systems."

9. As its title suggests, Ralph Ellison's 1955 essay "Living with Music" explores the unusual, unexpected, and under-discussed ways in which music interacts with daily life, and vice

versa. So why has the ever-present, extra-musical aspect of listening largely evaded or been ignored by (non-John Cageophile) critics and reviewers?

10. Marvin Bell and Christopher Merrill recently published a book of poetic correspondence, *After the Fact: Scripts & Postscripts* (2016), whose working title was *Everything at Once.* Isn't that a great mantra—"Everything at once"—for an ideal method of listening?

11. Without the five-note opera-house bell that informed his audience to please find their seats, Keith Jarrett would never have "composed" the indelible opening phrase to *Köln Concert* (1975).

12. Boone's *The Poetry of Jazz* opens with "Gin"—a long swig of it for our late-lamented Philip Levine—and the tune's head, with its flat-fives and harmonic-minor trills, is appropriately celebratory. I listen as I tidy around the house this morning, and gradually I observe a swagger in my step, a wanna-be-cool energy that echoes the poem's youth, comedy, eagerness, naiveté—all of which are on display from Levine's opening tip: "The first time I drank gin / I thought it must be hair tonic."

13. The first time I read a Levine poem I thought it must've been written by a friend's dad or somebody. So down-to-earth it was, so straight-talking. "You stand in the rain in a long line / waiting at Ford Highland Park. For work," begins "What Work Is," probably his most famous poem. Only years

later, in college, when I began to write poems myself, did I understand that Levine's disarming colloquialism was one of his greatest strengths.

14. Madhubuti, too, is disarming—differently. On most tunes, Mitchell's band lays a groove like a big quilt spread for a picnic, and Madhubuti recites. He doesn't recite his poems melodramatically or with oracular fever/fervor. To the contrary, he recites with a clear and measured humility. Almost a majesty. "The minor cadences of despair change often to triumph and calm confidence," wrote W.E.B Du Bois of "The Sorrow Songs." I believe *Liberation Narratives* is much closer to the "The Sorrow Songs" than first meets the ear.

15. But don't get me wrong: there *is* drama, musical excitement. Like a solo full of risk and surprise, listeners of *Liberation Narratives* experience a reaffirmation of the impulses that led to the formation and continual reformation of jazz in the first place—impulses to challenge, expand, resist, and give the slip to dominant Western rhythmic and harmonic expectations.

16. Jazz, after all, arose not from a mere desire to be "different" or "in vogue," but rather from deep personal, social, and cultural unrest, from a desire to transform the musical boundaries that reflect and stand in as a microcosm for the boundaries created by society itself. Just as citizen-subjects challenge normative conventions in the world, so jazz musicians challenge normative conventions in their music.

The Pleasure of Regret

Scott Manley Hadley

30/10/2020

like a pansexual roger moore

For my secondary education, I attended a grammar school.

A grammar school is a state (i.e. not private) school that students have to pass a test to attend.

Grammar schools were introduced to the UK with the idea that they would improve social mobility, but they didn't. By the time I began high school they had been phased out in the majority of the country.

I was one of the poorest students in all my classes.

For the last two years of high school, my grammar school became open to anyone who wanted to sit A levels, the exams you need to pass to attend university. My school year was about to be expanded by hundreds and hundreds of strangers: those who'd failed the grammar school entry exam and those who hadn't taken it.

There would be fresh blood.

I spent the summer imagining the friends I'd make.

I wanted leather jackets, cigarettes and hip-flasks;

I wanted indie rock and promiscuity;

I wanted eyes-open cosmopolitans;

I wanted lesbians and gays, poets and artists;

I wanted gorgeous, unattainable studs with the street smarts of the rougher school down the road and a fuck-it attitude to life;

I wanted

cool.

I wanted someone who talked about Flaubert, fellatio and fucking awesome parties.

I wanted an idol.

I wanted a hero.

I wanted a muse.

I wanted – and I got – Frank DuBois.

Frank DuBois arrived with a bang.

Frank brought hipflasks of his dad's whiskey into school.

Frank was a pack-a-day smoker and had been since he was fourteen.

Frank was tall and thin and **hairy**.

Frank had chest hair, aged sixteen!

Frank had a beard!

Frank had been the go-to-booze-buyer in his social circles since he was **thirteen**, puberty having hit him hard, fast and young.

Frank wanted liquor, Frank wanted women, Frank wanted luxury and Frank wanted adoration.

Frank wanted to project the image that I had hoped to find.

We were a perfect match.

Before we spoke, I thought Frank was aloof.

Frank was cast as the lead in the school play, which I'd fucking wanted. Once I got to know him, though, I understood.

He is – and always will be – a leading man.

He is – and was – charismatic.

At least, he is when he tries…

My Coleridge

Stephanie Limb

30/10/2020

To a Little Weanling Babe, who returned a kiss with great eagerness

Pretty Babe, 'tis all in vain,
Thou may'st suck and suck again,
But the lip, though soft it be,
Is no fount of milk for thee.
Baby, no! 'tis soft as silk,
But yet has nought to do with milk;
From the banks, where roses grow,
Lily streams shall never flow.

Baby when at man's estate,
Thou, with youthful hopes elate,
Seekest all things else above
Lady's fluent words of love;
Ne'er may lip, whence oft in dreams,
Flow for thee those nectar streams,
Dry as bloomless desart prove
When thou askest love for love. [39]

On breastfeeding

Breastfeeding doesn't turn me on but my nipples have always been part of sex. I find sex frustrating when I'm producing milk because this part of my body – a part that has always been linked to orgasms – is now assigned a different role. My nipples are cut off. My body is confused. I am a magician's assistant in a black box – cut in

magician waves a wand – to give me back my body. Motherhood owns the body so completely – it blocks all other feeling. This annihilation frightens me.

After four months, I try to give up breastfeeding Ted. I'm forced out of the house when my husband gives him that first bottle. He won't take it from me. He keeps rooting against my breast – mouth twisting and gumming the air. I go upstairs and listen to him wail through the bedroom floor. My body responds and my nipples buzz. The milk starts to come – they call this 'let down.' Apt. My top is soaked. I leave the house and sit in the car, weeping. I'm told that Ted cried himself to sleep.

In the middle of the night, when he cries for a night feed, my nipples drench the bed. I'm wearing breast pads but the milk pours – the mattress is soaked. Ted can smell my sweet yoghurty fug. My body radiates it. He can't understand why I won't give him my nipples. He throws his head backwards and forwards. Headbutts my chest. I waver. My breasts throb. Veins of milk bulge under the skin. The midwife said it was up to me. The NHS are militantly pro-breast – the benefits of breastfeeding *probably* outweigh the risks from the medication that passes through my milk. After that first night, I decide on a mid-course. The next evening, I give Ted a long bedtime feed. I take my pills. I sleep. I pump and dump the contaminated milk when I wake up. We replace it with formula. I repeat this process when Sid is born. I don't like the thought of someone else feeding them. Not even their dad. I am selfish. I am territorial. The midwives try to reassure me.

Sara weaned Edith early. At two months. She was convinced her milk was no good for Edith.

My nervous debility and other unpleasant symptoms increased so much that I was obliged to think seriously of feeding my darling E. She now takes milk and oats with a little sugar in it out of the bottle. She was frightened by the spoon and at first there was some repugnance of the bottle – but she now takes it very well in general.[40]

Sara worried about how she would balance motherhood and intellectual life before she got married. She wrote, 'no one should quarrel with a woman devoting her leisure to literary pursuits instead of using it in making knick knacks or at the piano or with the pencil'[41] and 'if less worthy amusements were given up I believe almost every woman might devote some time to books.'[42] When Sara's mother moved in with her after Herbert's birth, she wrote:

You cannot imagine how odd the change in Sara's habits appear to me – so different to those of her maiden days. Reading, writing, walking, teaching, dressing, mountain-eering, and I may add, for the latter 10 years of that state – weeping – were her daily occupations with occasional visiting – Now, house orders, suckling, dress and undress – walking, sewing – morning visits and receiving – with very little study of Greek, Latin and English (no weeping!) make up ... her busy day.[43]

Sara resumed weeping in 1832. Sara's weeping allowed her time to study. Sara wrote most of *Phantasmion* during a prolonged stay in Ilchester – she aborted her journey home (from the in-laws in Ottery St Mary) – sent the children back with the nurse and refused to move. By giving up breastfeeding – and taking up weeping – she was allowed time away from the children. In this poem she insists that her lips have 'nought to do with milk.' Words cannot nourish a baby. She separates the intellectual from the mother. Hilary Marland raises the question of 'how far it is possible for Sara to have "learned" her illness' and suggests that her illness 'may have provided the framework for her escape from maternal duties to resume her writing.'[44] This makes it sound calculated, as though she was feigning illness. I'm repeatedly told that anxiety is part of the body's 'fight, flight or freeze' response to stress. The body wants to find safety. Books make me feel safe too.

When my nervousness comes on, I look for books. I chain-read. I light a new book with the smouldering nub of the last. I've always read compulsively but when I feel panic, I absorb myself in book after book. Reading is my only relief. People suggest watching a film or listening to music but reading works – those other activities are passive. I need something active. I can't let my mind walk away. I wonder how much my response is learned. How much my response to stress is, these days, a way of escaping motherhood?

In the second stanza this poem performs a volta. The poem addresses a boy. Sara had no trouble breastfeeding her son, Herbert – but the tangled relationship with literature and breast milk is cast onto advice for a young man. In 1843 Henry died, Sara became close friends – soon after – with the poet Aubrey De Vere. He was twelve years younger than Sara. Sara sent this poem to De Vere and entered it into her red manuscript book under 'Poems for De Vere.' In this context the first stanza takes on another dimension: it becomes more playful – mocking, even: 'Stop rooting against my lips, baby. There's no milk. All I have is words.'

According to Klein's object relations theory the breast is the first object of desire. The child needs to understand that the breast is attached to a person and doesn't exist for his pleasure, alone. However, all future pleasure will be measured against that first breast. 'These lips have nought to do with milk, De Vere. You won't find your mother's breast in my mouth.' Sara's not interested in lactophilia or becoming a mother figure. Breastfeeding doesn't turn her on. Sara's advice to the young man – both Herbert and De Vere: 'Don't forget – *everything* that comes from a woman's mouth is hollow. Only milk can be trusted – but, *come damn it* – my milk is gone!' This woman is losing her son. This woman is aging.

I think about mothers and sons a lot. Perhaps that's why I am drawn to this poem. I have two sons. I won't have any more children (I sprung a coil into my uterus as soon as Sid was born). My sister tells me that mothers with sons (and no daughters) are deranged – unbalanced. We over-attach. Sara had a daughter – was therefore, more rational than me. I, with my two sons, will turn into my mother-in-law. No-one will be good enough for my boys. I don't want to be the mad mother who clings to her babies – scared that another woman will displace me from the centre of their lives. I suspect that I already am that mother – glimpsed in the second stanza of this poem.

Sara's 'bloomless desart' contrasts with the 'banks where roses grow.' The mouth of the woman is barren when the boy gives love and expects love in return. I'm reminded that a woman has two mouths. Two sets of lips. Her words cannot nourish. Her vagina cannot either. Sara is emphasising sterility. Let's read the poem again, looking at that other set of lips speaking to a young lover from beneath her skirt. From inside her pants – 'Thou may'st suck and suck again,/ But the lip, though soft it be,/ Is no fount of milk for thee.' No young beau can extract cyprine – quintessence – from Sara's vagina. Maybe this mucky reading takes the poem a step too far, but Sara wasn't a buttoned up Victorian daughter. She was the daughter of STC.

> There are some of my Father's Poems which, though racy and energetic, are not *drawing roomy*. I would not call them, or any part of them, *coarse*, for this is to stigmatize them, which I would not do; for I consider them within the allowable range of a *man's* pen, and can hardly think it is to be decided that nothing is to be written and printed which it could not be good manners to read aloud in mixed company. The exceeding fastidiousness of the present age, one part of it at least, is more a sign of effeminacy and *luxurious* delicacy than of purity, as it seems to me.[45]

To Sara, STC's 'racy' language is not coarse, or *locker roomy* (to translate her into twenty-first century speak) – she was irritated by the censorship of her era. She considers all STC's poems 'within the allowable range of a *man's* pen.' For me, a poem that welds the grief of abandoning breastfeeding to the anxiety of losing a son and the fantasy of sex with a younger man, is within the 'allowable range of a *woman's* pen' – even a *Victorian* woman's pen.

Living in Disneyland

Alex Mazey

30/10/2020

Are we Living in Disneyland?

A shallow interpretation of our consumerism today maintains that we are all given an 'illusion of choice'. *Coca-Cola* is Republican, and *Pepsi* is Democrat, with this key conceptualisation of politics as soft drinks pertaining that either choice is bad for you. However, it's precisely that choice of substituting one product for another that, in turn, develops our identity from the culture of significance that holds us captive. These choices are not academic or theoretical, but rather represent the day to day, unconscious desires of our ego, pertaining to how we would like to be represented to the outside world. In short, we find representation in our commodities because of this very reliance on sign-value.

What if I said *Perrier's Citron Lemon-Lime* and Perrier's *Pamplemousse Rose* both exist to supplement the illusion of *Perrier Natural*, similar to how *This Juicy Water* exists to imply *Evian Water* as a healthy, natural alternative? Of course, no choice is authentically natural, here – or healthy – but rather each a 'product' or 'commodity' with its own ideological significance. While it is commonly accepted that new commodities are continuously introduced to the market to offer more choice, hyperreality actually suggests that new products exist to sustain the illusion of a company's flagship commodity, which when viewed in isolation would become another nonsensical abstraction.

These choices are extended to our aesthetic tastes, which have become increasingly absorbed by this system of signs, as laid out by Jean Baudrillard in '*The System of Objects*'. This is what makes consumerism so alluring to us; it is not just a world of cheap illusions where the masses have been duped by some monstrous corporation, but rather an appeal to our base instincts, our selfish desires for some narcissistic gratification. In many ways, these techniques attempt to fulfil a spiritual emptiness.

In '*American Psycho*', when Patrick Bateman demonstrates his inner resentment at his colleague's superior business card, he knows he has been out-done by a 'tasteful thickness' – crushingly defeated – in this game of signs and signifiers, especially in regards to his own failed representation as the most powerful man in the room. In many ways, we all operate like Patrick Bateman looking to compete with our neighbours over the picket fences of our own egos. The power of our system lies in how it promotes not only the material successes of the uncompromising capitalist but also the moral virtue of the revolutionary activist.

Do we really believe that the same companies that led to ecological devastation – and historical oppression of the wage-earner – suddenly care about educated children and deforestation? In reality, there is no 'they care' but rather 'we care'. In the modern world, advertisement understands the importance of customer satisfaction, and there's nothing more economically satisfying than peddling the moral virtue that helps a consumer sleep at night. And so, consumers buy *Ben & Jerry's ice cream*, not to fuel an addiction to sugar, but rather to relive the victories of emancipation. This progressive idea of a separation between the conscious and unconscious consumer is yet another fiction in the game of hyperreality.

Perhaps, a more thematically relevant example of our unconscious states of hyperreality could be taken from a film like Gore Verbinski's *'A Cure for Wellness'*. Despite becoming a hugely unsuccessful, box-office failure, this psychological horror shows us the pervasive effects of nefarious illusions, negated only by a protagonist increasing his conscious state to one of heightened awareness. From the outset, the film follows the journey of a young business executive as he travels to a hydropathy clinic located in the atmospheric gothique of the Swiss Alps. Emblematic of the youthful, precarious accomplishments of a vague capitalist America, our troubled protagonist, Lockhart, is tasked with bringing home an increasingly estranged CEO, Roland Pembroke; who must face the criminal charges of corporate misconduct.

We observe Lockhart leaving the tangible, materialist world of financial services before ascending towards the mysterious, phantasmagorical realms of Dr Heinreich Volmer's 'wellness centre', where patients drink spring water imbued with a miraculously restorative property. Unable to locate Pembroke at the clinic, Lockhart is told by a mysterious girl that 'nobody ever leaves' and an accident later renders him to the status of 'patient'. Here, Lockhart begins his journey of mental deliquescence, increasingly unable to distinguish what's real and what isn't.

Of course, unlike the passive viewership, Lockhart soon discovers the dark truth of his own world; that is, despite ingesting large quantities of the spring water, the patients are suffering from profound dehydration. What was promised as a cure to the ailments of the modern world, actually exasperated the issues of his own 'depleted immune system', whereby all patients were made increasingly sick under the pretence of a cure. What's more, the water is distilled through the patients to produce a life-giving essence, that vastly

extends the natural lives of Dr Heinreich Volmer, his staff, and the mysterious girl, Hannah, whom Lockhart gradually befriends through some awkward romantic interaction.
Similar to this fiction, the system of signs is sustained by the distillation process of consumption, an essence that grows stronger through each generational proliferation – an everlasting quintessence. (It is no coincidence that the evil, manipulative characters' lives in '*A Cure for Wellness*' are unnaturally sustained through the sweat and willing ignorance of their victims.) Isn't this exactly how a neoliberal, capitalist realism works? The pervasive, technocratic advances of the future presented to us as tangible solutions, despite bringing a level of fatal, life-draining suffering and environmental degradation; a profundity sustained by our blind acceptance of a universal framework; a diagnosis we didn't need – our cure for wellness.
Following the defeat of Dr Volmer, the wellness clinic is burnt to the ground through the illuminating grandeur of arson. The surviving patients look on at the wreckage with the warped, existential angst of a fallen system. Meanwhile, Lockhart returns to a secondary, global world of illusion; that is, into the remnants of the hyperreal dystopia from which he came. Hannah clutches to him on the back of a bike, representing not only her freedom but perhaps her saviour's newfound perspective, a clarity beyond nihilism. And while Lockhart has rescued Hannah from her own perverse, corrupt, illusionary world, we wonder if Hannah will rescue Lockhart from his. The real story of a fiery revolution begins here, in the manic face of a corporate lackey.
Miguel F. Doria at the Centre for Environmental Risk at the University of East Anglia, produced a white paper in 2006,

titled *'Bottled water versus tap water: understanding consumers' preferences.'* According to Doria's research, 'a relatively large proportion of bottled water (between 40–60% globally) consists of packaged tap water[.]' Unsurprisingly enough, Doria's research revealed that 'from a strictly objective perspective, bottled water is not necessarily "better" or "worse" than tap water[...]' despite a schism in 'the media and scientific literature' regarding 'the merits and faults of each alternative.' While Doria's research provides a good overview of the general scientism, the paper reads with a subtle disingenuity, especially in regards to explaining the diverse possibilities 'for the increase of bottled water consumption.' According to his research, organoleptic reasons – the poor taste of tap water – was often given as an example of why people preferred bottled water. This is fascinating as it indicates the general milieu of the consumerist culture looking for satisfaction in everything, including the vital hydration of their bodies. The maintenance of one's health and wellbeing are almost used continuously as an opportunity for some cursory gratification. It seems the consumer will always view tap water in relation to the sugary delights of an ice-cold, *Coca-Cola.* This is an ideal representation of the Baudrillardian system of signs at work. Moreover, we can extend this analysis to other areas of our lives.

All breakfast cereals are competing with the appeal of an extra twenty minutes in bed; hence the proliferation of a market based on high-sugar products that appeal to both convenience and 'great taste', whilst also promoting a dialectic of natural authenticity. The task of preparing early morning sustenance is often presented as a task of dissatisfaction as if gratification should be the object of all our daily endeavours.

This warped, consumerist mentally is almost always present in advertisements and marketing; for example, where gyms promote vanity and personal aesthetics, over health and well-being. (Interestingly enough, even contraception promotes sensation over safety.)

Even so, a great deal of marketing offers to share in this illusion of health and wellbeing by externalising the abstraction to the abstract lives of other people. When we visit the supermarket, we will buy coffee regardless, feeding unhealthy yet necessary and urgent addictions to stimulants and sugar. Despite this horror, we can, at the very least, share in the warm fuzzies felt by the beneficiaries of fair trade, forest regrowth, etc. It seems coffee companies are now more than happy to present the illusion of opportunity and wellbeing for the future of its wage-earners. Of course, this is all done to conceal a purchase based on our own, shallow gratification.

Many consumers would like to believe this doesn't apply to them. They'd say, 'if coffee suppliers weren't ethical, I simply wouldn't buy the coffee'. If this is you, ask yourself, why doesn't this ethical virtue ever extend to the technology in your pocket or the clothes on your back? Along these lines, I suspect we will soon see the emergence of 'Ethical Technologies'; phones made by smiling faces, rather than, say, the child-slaves of the present day. This isn't a particularly revolutionary insight but rather another opportunity to point out how an abstract product; that is, coffee itself, absorbs yet another layer of abstraction, augmenting its chain of sign-value significance beyond mere societal prestige, elevating itself, ergo the consumer, with an additional sense of moral virtue.

On a Highstreet of cellophane sandwiches, soymilk lattes and pseudo-healthy choices, *Burger King* becomes a revolutionary experience of pure ideological desire. Here, products that are sold as health foods elsewhere are sold with a true-faced manifestation of their genuine depravity. The vegan activists campaigning outside offer an alternative vision that seems perhaps even more alienating and post-material than the industrial-scale, brutal slaughter of animals. This conceals the animus of veganism as perhaps another heightened sense of moral virtue against the masses; after all, what's saving animals against the spiritually fulfilling melodrama of resentment? Even so, Highstreet activism gets two things right: the comfort of crotch drops and analysis of legality as a product of power.

Ironically, healthy alternatives are almost always accompanied by *Coca-Cola*. A drink hardly ever criticised, but rather where cutting analysis is outsourced to the means by which the liquid is transmitted from can to mouth. I imagine the controversy surrounding plastic straws is almost entirely an attempt to avoid the criticism of the products themselves.

Philip K. Dick provides a vital conclusion, here: "Fake realities will create fake humans. Or, fake humans will generate fake realities and then sell them to other humans, turning them, eventually, into forgeries of themselves. So, we wind up with fake humans inventing fake realities and then peddling them to other fake humans. It is just a gigantic version of Disneyland."

Rhinoceros

Luke Thompson

30/10/2020

The Prehistory of Ganda

The Bible

The Bible is full of unicorns. Sort of. That is, the Biblical Hebrew *re'em* was translated into the Greek *monoceros*, which was then translated into the Latin *unicornus*, which was then translated into the English *unicorn*. And so we find English Bible translations packed with unicorns. There is lots of lovely debate about whether this is really a rhinoceros, an auroch, a kind of ox or something else altogether, and different Bibles translate the word in all sorts of ways.

Numbers 24:8

God brought him forth out of Egypt; he hath as it were the strength of an unicorn: he shall eat up the nations his enemies, and shall break their bones, and pierce them through with his arrows.

Deuteronomy 33:17

His glory is like the firstling of his bullock, and his horns are like the horns of unicorns: with them he shall push the people together to the ends of the earth: and they are the ten thousands of Ephraim, and they are the thousands of Manasseh.

Job 39:9-10

Will the unicorn be willing to serve thee, or abide by thy crib?
Canst thou bind the unicorn with his band in the furrow? or will he harrow the valleys after thee?

Psalm 92:10

But my horn shalt thou exalt like the horn of an unicorn

Diodorus (1st Century BCE)
The Library of History

(CH Oldfather translation, published by Loeb Classical Library, 1935)

At the tip of its nostrils it carries a horn which may be described as snub and in hardness is like iron. Since it is ever contesting with the elephant about pasturage it sharpens its horn on stones, and when it opens the fight with this animal it slips under its belly and rips open the flesh with its horn as with a sword. By adopting this kind of fighting it drains the blood of the beasts and kills many of them. But if the elephant has avoided the attempt of the rhinoceros to get under his belly and has seized it beforehand with his trunk, he easily overcomes it by goring it with its tusks and making use of its superior strength.

Martial (C.38-104AD)[1]
Epigrams

(Henry George Bohn translation, published by G. Bell and sons, 1897.)

On the Rhinoceros

The rhinoceros exhibited for thee, Caesar, in the whole space of the arena, fought battles of which he gave no promise. Oh, into what terrible wrath did he with lowered head blaze forth! How powerful was that tusk to whom a bull was a mere ball!

He who with armed nostril wildly glared,
Has fought the battles he had not declared.
How did his headlong rage the pit appal!
How flash'd the horn that made a bull a ball!

Elphinston

---

1 Martial was a first century Roman poet, known for his vast collection of 'epigrams'. Epigrams were an ancient Greek and Roman poetic genre, and Martial was a master of it, each short poem ending with a witticism or punchline.
In the translation favoured here, Henry George Bohn has first rendered the original text in prose and then paired it up with a poetic version by an English poet. Whenever they couldn't find a better poet, Bohn explains in his introduction, he hopes the reader will forgive him for having used the 'indifferent' poet Elphinston's verse. Elphinston's poetic translations of Martial were so bad that in an idle moment Robert Burns even mocked them:

O thou whom Poesy abhors,
Whom Prose has turned out of doors!
Heard'st thou yon groan? Proceed no further;
'Twas laurell'd Martial calling Murther!

Happily, all of the sections of Martial relating to the rhinoceros have Elphinston's murderous versionings.

On a Rhinoceros

While the trembling keepers were exciting the rhinoceros, and the wrath of the huge animal had been long arousing itself, the conflicts of the promised engagement were beginning to be despaired of; but at length his fury, well-known of old, returned. For easily as a bull tosses to the skies the balls placed upon *his horns*, so with his double horn did he hurl aloft the heavy bear.

While long they roused the hero to engage,
And bid his nostrils gather all their rage,
In vain the timid guides for battle burn'd;
When lo! the glory of his power return'd:
High a huge bear he heaved with double horn,
As a bull sends aloft the balls that brave his scorn.

Elphinston

LAY OUT YOUR UNREST

Lightning Source UK Ltd.
Milton Keynes UK
UKHW020646161120
373476UK00008B/225